Speaking of Ayurvedic Her Cures

Dr. T. L. Devaraj, M.D. in Ayurveda, is the author of 15 books on Ayurveda and its Ayurvedic remedies for common diseases. Several thousand copies of this book has been exported to the erstwhile U.S.S.R.

He is the recipient of an international award for his contribution to Ayurveda worldwide.

He has contributed several research papers in scientific journals on Ayurveda and has attended several national and international seminars on Ayurveda.

Currently, he is the Deputy Director of Ayurveda in the State of Karnataka.

Ayurveda for Healthy Living went into its 4th edition in a short time and it was exported to Spain and translated into the Spanish language. His another book, *Mane Maddu*, also went into its 4th edition. *Pancha Karma Treatment of Ayurveda*, exported worldwide, is being published in its 2nd edition.

Published by
Sterling Publishers Private Limited

Speaking of
Ayurvedic
Herbal Cures

T. L. DEVARAJ

A Sterling Paperback

STERLING PAPERBACKS
An imprint of
Sterling Publishers (P) Ltd.
L-10, Green Park Extension, New Delhi-110016
Ph.: 6511784, 6511785 Fax: 91-11-6851028
E-mail: sterlin.gpvb@axcess.net.in

Speaking of Ayurvedic Herbal Cures
©1997, T.L. Devaraj
ISBN 81 207 1863 1
Reprint 1998

All rights are reserved. No part of this publication may be reproduced,
stored in a retrieval system or transmitted, in any form or by any
means, mechanical, photocopying, recording or otherwise, without
prior written permission of the publisher.

Published by Sterling Publishers Pvt. Ltd., New Delhi-110016.
Lasertypeset by Surya Computer Services, New Delhi.
Printed at Ram Printograph (India), Delhi-110051.
Cover design by Narendra Vashishta

In the memory of
My Beloved Son
Late T. D. Srinivasa

FOREWORD

I am glad to write a foreword to a book entitled *Speaking of Ayurvedic Herbal Cures* by Dr. T. L. Devaraj, eminent Ayurvedic Physician and former Professor and Head of the Department of Dravyaguna and Panchakarma, Government College of Indian Medicine, Mysore; and Principal, Government Taranatha Ayurveda Medical College, Bellary. Presently, he is the Deputy Director of Ayurveda, Karnataka State. He has written fifteen books on Ayurveda. And three of his books are recognised by the Central Council of Indian Medicine, New Delhi. He is the first Kannadiga to get three of his books included in the Syllabus of Ayurvedic courses by the Central Council of Indian Medicine, New Delhi. He had been honoured for his outstanding contributions to Ayurveda by Jagadguru Abhinava Vidyatirtha Swamiji of Sharada Peetham, Sringeri, Karnataka State and Madhya Pradesh Government, and Ayurveda Prachara Parishad of Karnataka State.

The present book, *Speaking of Ayurvedic Herbal Cures*, deals with herbs and their properties and important therapeutic uses. The illustrations are inserted in this work to facilitate the identification of the herbs by any reader. The nutritive value of some of the drugs and the dosage of each drug are also mentioned.

I hope, therefore, that this work would be useful for both the common man and for the practitioners of the different systems of medical sciences.

I wish the book and the author every success.

D. Javare Gowda
Former Vice-Chancellor,
Mysore University,
Mysore

PREFACE

I am pleased to present this book to the readers, as it has given me a splendid opportunity to share these nuggets of information on Ayurveda. The diseases which have been earlier treated with other systems of medicine, have side effects besides being costly and not within the reach of the common people. So the centres of Ayurveda are being established in America, Japan, Germany and other parts of the world.

Ayurveda was conceived in India by the grace of Brahma, the creator of the universe. In the present volume, individual herbs for each disease are presented with their dosage. Treatment for 75 diseases have been dealt with, for the benefit of our readers. The illustrations of the plants have also been given to facilitate easy identification before their use. The names of the herbs are listed in different languages, so that they are understood by different sections of the people.

The herbs which are mentioned in the book, are in the central syllabus of BAMS, the Ayurveda degree course. Hence this book would be of great help to them.

This book is not only useful for common people but also for the practitioners of Ayurveda and other systems of medicine.

I am highly indebted to Sri Javare Gowda former vice-chancellor of Mysore University for having written a Foreword to this publication. I am also thankful to Sterling Publishers for having brought out this book well in time.

T.L. Devaraj

CONTENTS

CONTENTS

ADENITIS

Adenitis is nothing but inflammation of the glands in the neck. This gives pain and discolouration and swelling of the adenous region. The main glands involved are the adenoids. The bark of the drug *Kovidara* is used as a decoction as well as an external application.

Kovidara is also called *Red Mandara*. It grows all over India. Its bark and flowers are used in medicines.

It is of three varieties, depending on the colour of its flowers:

1. White *Kovidara*

                                  2. Yellow *Kovidara*
                                    3. Red *Kovidara*.

The names of this drug in different languages are:

Sanskrit--*Kovidara*, Kannada--*Kanchuvala*, Hindi--*Kachannar*, Telugu--*Devakran Channamu*, Tamil--*Segapu Menthari*, Latin--*Bauhinia variegata*, English--*Camel's foot tree*.

Properties: It has an astringent taste.

Uses: It cures the wounds or ulcers in case of scrofula and adenitis. Its powder must be applied externally and its decoction must be given internally.

Dosage: Bark powder 2-4 gms per day.
Flower powder 1-2 gms per day.

ANASARCA

Anasarca is swelling all over the body. It may be due to hypo-protenaemia and anaemia or due to any other cause. The use of the *Shigru* fruit in the form of fruit or leaves in diet is very useful and prevents oedema all over the body.

Shigru is otherwise called *Shobhanjana*.

The names of this drug in different languages are:
Sanskrit--*Shigru*, Kannada--*Nuggegida*, Hindi--*Shijan*, English--*Drumstick*, Telugu--*Hunaja*, Tamil--*Hurangi*, Latin--*Moringa olifera*.

It grows all over India. Its bark, seeds, leaves and oil are all used in medicines and also in the diet.

Its composition of 100 gms:

1. Vitamin A   - 10,000 I.U.
2. Vitamin B_2 - 58 mgm
3. Vitamin C   - 216 mgms
4. Carbohydrate   - 13 gms
5. Fat   - 1½ gms
6. Protein   - 5 gms
7. Phosphorus   - 60 mgms
8. Calcium   - 400 gms
9. Iron   - 6 mgms

Properties: It has a bitter and pungent taste. It is hot in potency.

Uses: It is used both as an item of diet and as a medicine.

Dosage: Its powder is used in doses of 5-10 grains and its decoction is used in a dosage of ½ to 1 ounce.

Shigru

ANOREXIA

Anorexia is a state of lack of appetite in a person. Without a proper appetite one cannot have the desire for eating.

Lemon grows all over India, especially in Bombay, Bengal, Burma and Assam. Its fruit and juice are used in medicines, and widely used in cooking, pickles, etc.

The names of this drug in different languages are:

Sanskrit–*Nimbooka*, Kannada–*Nimbehannu*, Hindi–*Kagajanimbulpu*, Telugu–*Nimmapandu*, Tamil--*Elumicchai*, Latin–*Citrus medica acida*, English–*Lemon of India*.

It is of two types, depending on its size:
1. Small
2. Big.

100 gms of lemon is composed of:
1. Vitamin A   - A small quantity
2. Vitamin B_1 - 19 mcg
3. Vitamin B_2 - 1¼ mcg
4. Vitamin B_6 - 0.5 mcg
5. Vitamin C   - 60 mgms
6. Potassium   - 160 mgms
7. Sulphur   - 11 mgms
8. Magnesium   - 10.5 mgms
9. Calcium   - 105 mgms
10. Carbohydrate   - 8 mgms
11. Protein   - 1.0 mgm
12. Sodium   - 5.5 mgms

Properties: It has a pungent taste and hot potency.

Uses: It is used in the treatment of vomiting and also in constipation. The big sized lemon (king lemon) also has an acidic and sweet taste and it helps to digest the food. It is good for bile and nervous disorders.

ANAEMIA

Anaemia may be due to different causes, like malnutrition or other diseases. *Tarkari* is one of the herbs used in Ayurveda for effective treatment of anaemia.

Tarkari grows all over India. Its root and bark are used in medicines.

Its names in different languages are:

Sanskrit--*Tarakari*, Kannada--*Taggimara*, Hindi--*Ageita*, Telugu--*Takkali*, Tamil--*Erumainmullayi*, Latin--*Clerodendron phlomidis.*

It is of three types:
1. *Taggi* plant
2. *Nadega Vahnimentha*
3. *Vishapernari* plant.

Properties:	Hot potency and taste.
Uses:	It is effective in anaemia and in loss of appetite.
Dosage:	A dose of 15 to 30 ml *tarkari* effectively used with water followed by buttermilk.

APHRODISIAC — I

Man is a civilised person. He should take food only to combat hunger. So also he should satisfy his sex urge. Normally, every individual will have sexual instinct, from puberty onwards to the middle age. In extraordinary persons the sex potency will be seen even after middle age. Persons who are lacking in potency must

be prescribed drugs which are mentio-ned in the aphrodisiac group, i.e., *Ekshuraka* is one such drug which can be used alone or in combination with any drug which has the same property.

Ekshuraka grows in India nearby watery areas.

It is of two types depending on the colour of flowers:
1. White flower, and
2. Blue flower.

Its names in different languages are as follows:

Sanskrit--*Exshuraka,* Kannada--*Kolavelka,* Hindi--*Tala Makhana,* Telugu--*Niguritere,* Tamil--*Nirmali,* Latin--*Astercontha lengifolia.*

Properties:	The root, leaves, seeds and *Kshara* are used in medicine. *Ekshuraka* has a sweet taste and cold potency. Hence, it stops diarrhoea and increases the virilific power in the body and also alleviates phlegmatic diseases.
Uses:	Its leaves have sweet and bitter tastes. Its seeds are advised in stimulating sex urges.
Dosage:	1-2 gm lotus seeds with milk twice.

APHRODISIAC — II

An aphrodisiac requirement occurs at an age of 45 years and above in individuals, when ageing starts. A sweet variety of *Alabukam* is advocated and used to tone up the sex organs and muscles of the body.

It grows all over in India. Its roots, stem, flowers seeds, and

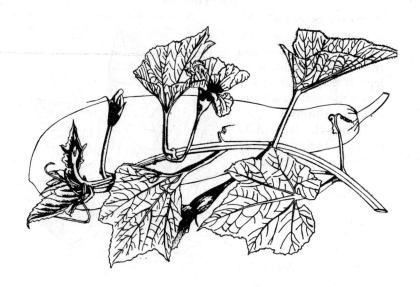

fruits are used in medicines.

In other languages its names are:

Sanskrit--*Alabukam,* Kannada--*Kahisore,* Hindi--*Lank,* Telugu--*Sorakayi,* Tamil--*Sorakayi,* Latin--*Lagenaria lecantha,* English--*Bittergourd.*

It is of two varieties:
1. Bitter
2. Sweet.

Properties: Bitter variety--Its seeds are indicated in difficulty in breathing.
Sweet variety--It is sweet in taste and unctuous in property. It is a tonic as it increases the virilific power of the body.

Uses: It is used in nervous disorders. It enhances strength in the body. It tones up muscles and nerves to give sexual strength.

Dosage: 1 to 2 gm with milk twice daily after food.

ARTHRITIS

Arthritis is caused by inflammation of the joints leading to acute pain and restricted movement of legs. It may occur at any age as rheumatoid arthritis or osteo-arthritis.

Deepyaka is widely grown in India, especially in Bombay. Only the seeds are used in prepa-ring medicines.

The names of this drug in different languages are:

Sanskrit--*Deepyaka,* Kannada--*Sanna Vadakki,* Telugu--*Omam,* Tamil--*Omam,* Latin--*Trachyspermumammi.*

100 gms of *Deepyaka* contains nutrients like
1. Carbohydrate – 37.2 gms
2. Protein – 14.8 gms
3. Fat – 16.5 gms
4. Calcium – 1300 mgms
5. Phosphorus – 288 mgms
6. Iron – 133 mgms

Properties: It has a bitter taste and is hot in potency.
Uses: It is extensively used in phlegmatic diseases. In the case of arthritis it is applied over the joint.
Dosage: It is used as *Ajamodadi arka*--5-15 drops with equal or double the quantity of water.

BAD ODOUR IN THE BODY

Bad odour in the body occurs due to improper hygienic conditions. But this can be avoided by taking regular baths and using washed, ironed clothes. This can also be to some extent remedied by using the decoction of *Krishna Mooli* and can also be applied on the body in the form of a powder. Its description is given below.

Krishna Mooli grows all over India generally and mostly in Kerala, Bombay, Bengal and Lanka. Only its root is used.

It is of two types:
1. Black *Krishna Mooli*
2. White *Krishna Mooli*.

Its names in different languages are:
Sanskrit--*Krishna Mooli*, Kannada--*Kariya Sogadeberu*, Hindi--*Anantamool*, Telugu--*Muktapulugam*, Tamil--*Naannari*, Latin--*Hemidesmus indicus*, English--*Black Indian Sarsaparilla*.

Properties:	Both varieties of *Krishna Mooli* are sweet in taste and cold in potency.
Uses:	It is used in treating offensive smell in the body. The powder of *Krishna Mooli* is applied on the body in the form of a paste. Its decoction can also be used.
Dosage:	1 to 2 gm with milk twice daily after meals.

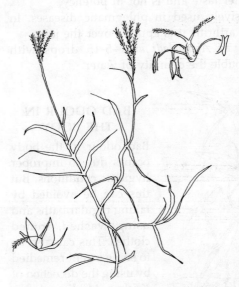

BLEEDING NOSE

Bleeding through the nose occurs in individuals, in children and adults, whenever there is vitiation of *pitta* in the body. But in the case of hypertension, bleed-ing from the nose occurs. *Shataparva* is an effective remedy. It can be instilled in the form of juice into the nose for instant relief.

Shataparva grows all over India. The entire plant is used in medicines.

Its names in different languages are as follows:
Sanskrit--*Shataparva*, Kannada--*Garikehullu*, Hindi--*Doot*, Telugu--*Doorvalu*, Tamil--*Arugompilu*, Latin--*Cynodon dactylon*, English--*Indian Beriberi*.

Shataparva is of five types:
1. Blue-coloured
2. White-coloured
3. *Ganda*
4. *Malla*
5. *Granthi.*

Properties: *Shataparva* has a bitter and sweet taste and is cold
                 in potency.
Uses: To stop bleeding from the nose.
Dosage: 5-10 drops of its juice must be inhaled.

BLOOD DISORDERS

We are living in the modern world and are in the habit of consuming more irritants and spicy, acrid and adulterated food at irregular intervals. This causes vitiation of the blood. For this purpose, *Raktasara* is the drug recommended not only to purify the blood, but also to improve the complexion of the person.

Raktakaggali is also named after the *Mriga Shira* tree.

Its names in different languages are as follows:

Sanskrit--*Raktasara*, Kannada--*Kempuk-aggali*, Hindi--*Khair*, Telugu--*Ponalmanu*, Tamil--*Chukatti*, Latin--*Acasia catechu*, English--*Catechu*

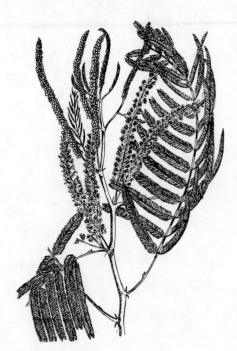

It is of five types:
1. White *Raktasara*
2. Red *Raktasara*
3. *Raktasara*
4. Black *Raktasara*
5. Offensive *Sara*.

Properties:	It is easily digestible and dry in nature. It is bitter and astringent in taste. In the final phase of digestion it becomes pungent. It has a cold potency.
Uses:	In treating skin diseases it is used effectively.
Dosage:	It is given in a dose of 1-2 gms of its powder and its decoction of 30 ml twice daily.

BRONCHIAL ASTHMA — I

Bronchial asthma is a disease of the lungs as per modern medicine. But according to the Ayurvedic system of medicine it starts from the stomach. In Ayurveda the main treatment lies in correcting the digestive system. The drug used is *Kantakari.*

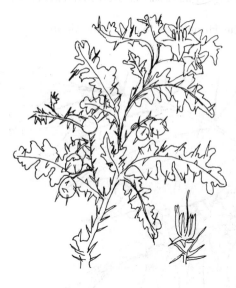

The names of *Kantakari* in different languages are:

Sanskrit--*Nidig-dhika*, Kannada--*Nela-gulla*, Hindi--*Bhatak-karraiah*, Telugu--*Vak-udu,* Tamil--*Kantakat-tari*, Latin--*Solanum xanthocarpum*, English--*Badam Janbery.*

Kantakari is grown in Bengal, Assam, Punjab, and in South India. Its leaves, bark, root, fruits are all used in medicines.

It is of four types:
1. *Kantakari*
2. *Laxmana*
3. *Kasghni*
4. *Vrintaki.*

Properties:	It has a pungent and bitter taste, is hot in potency and is widely used in the treatment of cough and bronchial asthma. It adds flavour to food, relieves,

fevers, nervous debility, and diseases due to indigestion.

Uses: It is given to relieve all types of coughs and dyspnoea, in the form of *Kantakari* decoction.

Dosage: For adults it should be given in a dose of one ounce with equal quantity of water at 6 a.m. and 6 p.m.

BRONCHIAL ASTHMA — II

Bronchial asthma is a condition wherein a person feels great difficulty in breathing. This is due to a spasm in the lungs. According to Ayurveda the disease starts from the stomach due to indigestion. *Karkataka Shrungi (Kuleeyaka)* is used extensively for treating this disease.

Kuleeyaka grows in the Himalayas, Nepal and Assam.

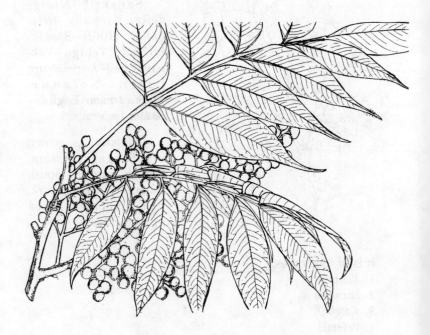

Its names in different languages are as follows:
Sanskrit--*Kuleeyaka*, Kannada--*Karkata Shrungi*, Tamil--*Kakkatti Shringi*, Latin--*Pistacia integerima*, English--*Madar*.

It is of two types:
1. *Karkataka Shrungi*
2. *Garshe Hambu.*

Properties:	It has a bitter and astringent taste.
Uses:	It alleviates cough, asthma and tuberculosis. When suffering from asthma, a patient should be given the seeds of *Moolaka* and *Karkataka Shrungi* along with honey.
Dosage:	½ to 2 gms per day.

BRONCHIAL ASTHMA — III

A patient gasps for breath due to anoxia in the lungs. *Sooryapushpi* is a drug of choice for this disorder. Its details are as follows:

Sooryapushpi is called the *Sravana-nakshatra* plant. This grows all over India.

Its names in different languages are:
Sanskrit--*Soorya-pushpi*, Kannada--*Ekkada gida*, Hindi–*Madaar*, Telugu–*Geludu*, Tamil--*Erakku*, Latin--*Calotropis procera*, English--*Madar*.

It is of four types:
1. Small variety of *Sooryapushpi*
2. Big variety of *Sooryapushpi*
3. White variety of *Sooryapushpi*
4. Red-flowered *Sooryapushpi*.

Properties: It is bitter and pungent in taste. It increases the digestive process, and helps in the proper assimilation of food.

Uses: The burnt ash of the leaves of this plant is effective in asthma.

Dosage: It should be taken in a dose of 3-15 grains to produce sweating in the body.

BILIOUS DISORDERS

Bilious disorders are very common due to the excessive use of pungent and irritant food items in the diet, like chillies, etc. *Varna Moolakam* is the drug of choice for such complaints.

Varna Moolakam is grown along the edges of rivers and is found in Rajasthan and Bengal. Only its roots are used.

Its names in different languages are:

Sanskrit--*Varna Moolakam*, Kannada--*Lamancha*, Hindi--*Khas*, Telugu--*Vetipara*, Tamil--*Elamacchai*, Latin--*Vetiveria zizanioides*, English--*Khaskhas grass*.

Properties: It has a cold potency and sweet and bitter taste.

Uses:	It is used in nervous and bilious disorders. It also increases one's strength.
Dosage:	1 to 2 gms of the powder of its root, twice daily before meals.

CHRONIC FEVER

Chronic fevers are due to very many reasons like tuberculosis, jaundice, indigestion, etc. The patient will be in a state of emaciation. In Ayurveda *Chinnaruha* is advocated for such conditions.

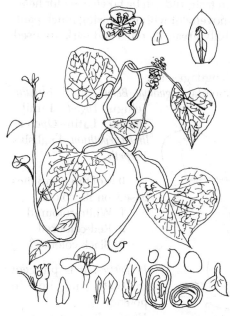

Chinnaruha grows all over India. It is a creeper. Its leaves and stem are used in medi-cines.

Its different names are:

Sanskrit--*Chinna-ruha,* Kannada--*Amrith-aballi,* Hindi--*Giloy,* Telugu--*Trippetige,* Tamil--*Sindalekodi,* Latin--*Tinospora cordi-folia,* English--*Gulancha.*

It is of two types:
1. *Kata Guduchi*
2. *Pindaguduchi.*

Properties: It has a bitter and astringent taste.

Uses: It can be effective in piles and skin diseases. In *vata* disorders its juice is given with ghee, in *pitta* disorders with sugar and in *kapha* with honey.

Dosage: In chronic fevers its juice of one ounce is given
                 with equal quantity of water twice daily, for a
                 period of 15 days to 1 month.

CONSTIPATION

Constipation is due to our civilised habit of eating less and
drinking coffee or tea too often. This can be a complication for
other diseases also, but it usually leads to piles. *Tribhandi* is
commonly used in Indian medicine to relieve constipation. It is a
powerful laxative and is used in the form of *lehyam* as *Trivrit
lehyam* which is very sweet in taste and can be taken even for heart
diseases. This helps bowel movement without causing much pain.

Tribhandi grows in the hilly areas. Its roots and bark are used
in medicines.

Its names in different languages are:
Sanskrit--*Tribhandi*, Kannada--*Tigadaya Beru*, Hindi--*Birodhi*,
Telugu--*Togad*, Tamil--*Shivadi*, Latin--*Operculina turpethum*, English--*Turpeth*.

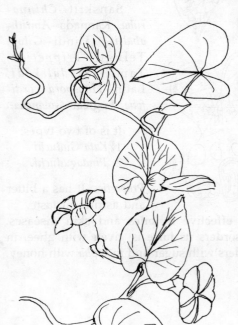

It is of three varieties
based on its colour.
1. White-coloured
2. Red-coloured
3. Black-coloured

Properties: It is pungent
in taste and hot in
potency.
Uses: It is used as a
purgative. In *Sharad Ritu*
(winter) the drug is
mixed with *Draksha* and
Atimadura for easy
movement of the
bowels. In all seasons
itcan be given with
Katuka. For chronic pain

cases it is used along with rock salt to produce purgation.

Dosage: 3 to 5 gms.

CONVULSIONS

These are nothing but violent muscular spasms in the body. This may occur either due to worms or due to complications caused by some diseases. There are some simple remedies in Ayurveda. One such is *Jaatikosha*. It is used in the form of a powder.

Jaatikosha is useful in the house as a remedy for many minor ills.

It is called by the following names in different languages:
Sanskrit--*Jaatikosha*, Kannada--*Jaayikayi*, Hindi--*Jaypal*, Telugu
--*Jaayikeya*, Tamil--*Jaadikayi*, Latin--*Myristica fragrans*, English--
Nutmeg.

The nutrients that are present in 100 gms of *Jaatiphala* are as
follows:

1. Vitamin A   - in small quantity
2. Protein   - 7 gms
3. Fat   - 28 gms
4. Carbohydrate   - 118 mgms
5. Phosphorous   - 230 mgms
6. Iron   - 11.9 mgms
7. Calcium   - 117 mgms

It grows in South India and Sri Lanka. It is of two varieties:
1. *Sugandha Jaayikayi* (Aromatic)
2. *Nirgandha Jaayikayi* (Non-aromatic).

Properties: It has an astringent and pungent taste. It has
                hot potency.
Uses: It is used in convulsions with positive benefit: The
                oil extract of *Jaatiphala* will alleviate convulsions in
                children and nervous diseases.
Dosage: 1 to 5 drops till the symptoms are alleviated.

CORYZA

Whenever there is any change in the climate or if any food which
is not suitable is taken, then the conditions will produce coryza.
For such a disease the use of pepper is very beneficial.

Mareecha (pepper) is grown in Kerala and the Malnad area of
Karnataka.

It is of two varieties depending on its colour:
1. Black Pepper and
2. White Pepper.

Its names in different languages are as follows:
Sanskrit--*Mareecha*, Kannada--*Menasu*, Hindi--*Kalimirch*,
Telugu--*Meriyalu*, Tamil--*Milagu*, Latin--*Piper nigrum*, English--*Black
Pepper.*

100 gms of pepper comprises:
1. Carbohydrate - 45 gms
2. Vitamin C - 24.5 gms
3. Calcium - 240 mgms
4. Phosphorus - 190 mgs
5. Iron - 15.5 mgsm
6. Fat - 5 mgms

Properties: It is pungent and bitter in taste and hot in potency. It becomes sweet in the final phase of digestion.

Uses: It increases and improves digestion, it relieves cough, asthma and phlegm. In phlegmatic coughs, simply chewing it will yield good results or else if it is taken with sugar-candy and honey it will be more beneficial. It cures syphilis, piles and spermatorr-hoea when it is used with *Bala Menasu.*
Dosage: 250 to 500 mg.

COUGH — I

Coughs are of two types, wet and dry cough. In all types of coughs with expectoration the use of either decoction or powder of *Twak* is recommended.

Twak grows in South India and the Himalayas. It is an aromatic drug used in our houses daily while preparing vegetable or mutton *biryani* or vegetable or mutton soup.

Its name in different languages are as follows:
Sanskrit--*Twak,* Kannada--*Dalchinni,* Hindi--*Dalchini,* Telugu--*Sanalipu,* Tamil--*Kararusha,* English--*Cinnamon,* Latin--*Cinnamomum zeylanicum.*

It is composed of sinnamic, urinol, pellandrin, terpeenete.

It is of three types:
1. *Chini* type
2. Ceylon type
3. Indian type.

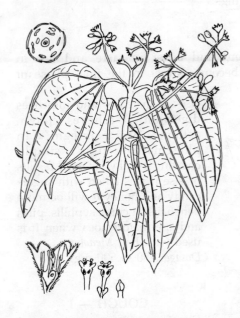

The bark of the plant is mainly used. Its leaves, bark, and oils are also used in medicines.

Properties: It has a sweet and pungent taste and cold potency.

Uses: It is used in treating heart, bladder and nasal disorders. It improves the colour of the skin. In rheumatic disorders and phlegm associated with nervous disorders it is effectively used. For loose motions associated with blood dysentery, cardamom, *twak* and ginger must be given along with honey; for influenza and typhoid fevers, it is given with a mixture of ginger, cardamom and cinnamon. It is used in many tooth powders as an aromatic drug. While treating for worms it acts as a vermicidal. It promotes digestion and purifies the blood. It is also used in the making of a drug to relieve pain during menstruation (dysmenorrhoea).

It cures phlegmatic and productive coughs. It also clears throat congestion.

Dosage: 150 to 600 mgms (powder) + honey.

COUGH — II

Coughs are seen to afflict all ages of people from an infant to an old man. It may be of the dry or wet type. Nowadays the use of antibiotics will control it to some extent. But the oral use of antibiotic usually produces deleterious effects on the intestinal flora which are very essential for the synthesis of vitamins in the body. So it is in the best interests of an individual who suffers from cough to take the powder of *Terminalia belerica.*

Karshapalam grows in India in its hilly areas.

It is of two types:
1. Small variety of *Karshapala.*
2. Big variety of *Karshapala.*

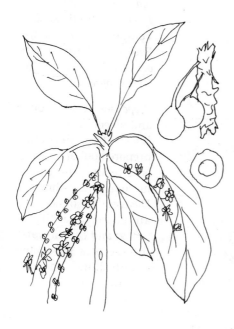

It has got different names in different languages as follows:

Sanskrit--*Karshapala*, Kannada--*Tare-kayi*, Hindi--*Baheda*, Telugu--*Tadikayi*, Tamil--*Akkoan*, Latin--*Terminalia belerica*, English--*Beleric myrobalan.*

Properties: Only its fruit is used. It has a pungent, bitter, astringent taste and hot potency. It is sweet in *vipaka.*

Dosage: It can be given in the treatment of coughs, in the form of a powder, in a dose of ½ to 1 gm with honey, twice daily.

COUGH — III

A cough is a symptom of many diseases including tuberculosis but in Ayurveda the cough is a disease by itself. There are several varieties of cough--with expectoration and without expectoration (wet and dry). Many cough syrups that are available do contain the drug *Kasamarda.* This is the drug of choice used solely to control the disease. It should be administered in the form of a decoction obtained out of its leaves.

Kasari grows in South India and in the Himalayas and Burma. Its roots, seeds and leaves are used in medicines.

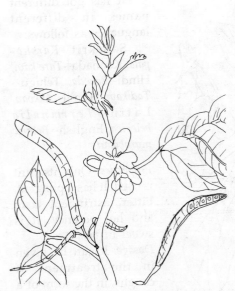

Its names in different languages are as follows:

Sanskrit--*Kasamarada*, Kannada--*Dodda Tagache*, Hindi--*Kasandi*, Telugu--*Kasda*, Tamil--*Pevarirai*, Latin--*Cassia occidentalis*, English--*Nigro coffee plant*.

Properties: It has a bitter and sweet taste.
Uses: The decoction prepared out of its leaves is effective, in cough, hiccups and asthma.
Dosage: One ounce with an equal quantity of boiled and cooled water. In case of a productive cough honey can be added.

COUGH — IV

Cough, especially when it is chronic, can be caused by tuberculosis. This can be relieved by the use of *Kuchaphalam*, that is, pomegranate fruit. The decoction of the fruit is taken along with other drugs.

Kuchaphalam grows all over in India and also in Africa and Iran.

Its names in different languages are:

Sanskrit--*Kuchaphala*, Kannada--*Dalimbhe Hannu*, Hindi--*Anar*, Telugu--*Dadima*, Tamil--*Modavai*, Latin--*Punica granatum*, English--*Pomegranate*.

Its composition of 100 gms is:
1. Vitamin A- 199% I.V.
2. Vitamin B$_2$- 199 mcg

3. Oxalic acid - 198 mcg
4. Phosphorus- 68 mgm
5. Calcium- 19 gms
6. Carbohydrate- 14 gms
7. Protein - 13 gms
8. Potassium -16 gms
9. Sodium - 3.5 gms

Properties: It is of two types, viz., sweet and acid. According to the place of origin and cultivation it is of four types: *Kabool, Chittamani, Kweta,* etc. It has a sweet, acidic and astringent taste, unctuous property and hot potency.

Uses: It is used to alleviate the *tridosha* of the body. It relieves the burning sensation in the body.

Dosage: In the case of tuberculosis the fruit in the form of decoction along with barley, ginger, horsegram and about 100 gms of goat mutton mixed in 4 cups of water is boiled and reduced to one cup. This should be administered in the morning at 11 a.m., only once in a day. This soup alleviates cough, headache, pain in the chest, burning sensation and the fever of tuberculosis.

1 to 2 ounces before the two main meals.

COUGH — V

A cough may be phlegmatic or dry. In both types *Surasa* is extensively used in India. It is used in the form of a decoction.

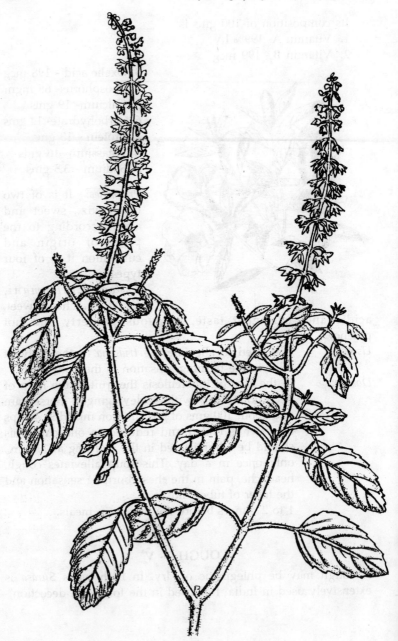

Surasa

Surasa is a well-known drug used for fever.

It grows all over India. It is of six types:
1. White *Tulasi*
2. Karpoora *Tulasi*
3. Black *Tulasi*
4. Sugandha *Tulasi*
5. Forest variety of *Tulasi*.

The different names in other languages are as follows:
Sanskrit--*Surasa*, Kannada--*Tulasi, Gida,* Latin--*Ocimum sanctum,*
English--*Holy Basil.*

Uses: It is used to relieve cough. It is also used in
             treating generalised oedema and phlegmatic
             diseases.

Dosage: The decoction of one ounce of *Tulasi* with an equal
             quantity of water, twice daily, is found to be
             effective in coughs.

DECREASED BREAST MILK

Breast milk is the best milk and is most suitable for infants. It is free from infection and is fresh and nutritious. The bottle-fed babies are easily prone to diseases. Modern ladies don't want the infants to be fed with their breast milk. This is highly deplorable and one should realise better late than never about the efficacy of breast milk. But for those ladies who wish to increase their breast milk, the use of cotton seed is advocated in Ayurveda. Even in the preparation of modern medicines for increasing the quantity of breast milk cotton seeds are used as a galactogogue.

Pichu is grown in all parts of India, especially in Karnataka, Bombay, Madras, Gujarat, and Bengal.

Its names in different languages are as follows:
Sanskrit--*Pichu*, Kannada--*Hathigida*, Hindi--*Kapas*, Telugu--*Patti*, Tamil--*Parutti*, Latin--*Gossypium herbaceus*, English--*Cotton plant*.

Properties:	It consists of a sweet and astringent taste, is light in action and hot in potency. So it alleviates *vata* disorders (neuromuscular disorders).
Composition:	Aminoacids like Methonian Tripteophone Pamitic, Stearic, Oleic and Vinolic acid are present.
Uses:	Its roots, flowers, bark and seeds are used in medicines. It is used as a galactogogue to produce breast milk.
Dosage:	1 to 2 gms with boiled, cooled milk.

DIABETES MELLITUS — I

Diabetes mellitus has become very common in this civilised world. This disease was known to us as early as three thousand years ago. We come across vivid descriptions of diseases in the ancient *Samhitas*, wherein they were using herbal remedies in treating this disease. *Kunchika*, a seed, is used in the treatment of diabetes. It is available as granules marketed by Dey's Pharmaceuticals as *Nosulin*.

Kunchika (Methi) grows all over India and is of two types:
1. The Medicinal variety
2. The Forest variety.

The following are the names in different languages:
Sanskrit--*Kunchika*, Kannada--*Mentya*, Hindi--*Methi*, Telugu--*Mentilu*, Tamil--*Vendayam*, Latin--*Trigonella foenum gracecum*.

Its compostion of 100 gms is as under:
1. Vitamin A - 6000 I.U.
2. Vitamin B_1 - 48 mcg.

3. Vitamin B$_2$ - 160 mcg.
4. Iron - 16 mgm.
5. Calcium - 440 mgms.
6. Fat - ¼ gms.
7. Protein - 3½ gms.
8. Carbohydrate - 9 gms.

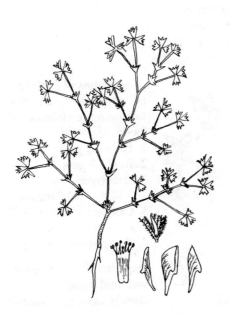

Properties: It is pungent and bitter in taste. It alleviates phlegm and fever, palliates cough, gout, worms and bacteria, skin diseases and nervous disorders. It increases the quantity of blood in the body.

Uses: It has proved to be an anti-diabetic, when used daily.

Dose: 1-5 gms with hot water.

DIABETES MELLITUS — II

Diabetes mellitus is a disease known to Indians more than three thousand years ago. In ancient compendiums like *Charaka* and *Susrutha*, sages have written about diabetes. It is nothing but *Madhu Meha*. For such a disease, to control excessive urination and hunger and to reduce high blood sugar, there are many drugs in Ayurveda. But *Phalendra* is very effective and it is present in most of the Ayurvedic medicines recommended for diabetes mellitus.

Phalendra (Jambooka) is also called Rohini Star Tree. It grows all over India.

Its names in different languages are as follows:
Sanskrit--*Phalendra*, Kannada--*Jum Nerala*, Hindi--*Jamoon*, Telugu--*Nered*, Tamil--*Shambu*, Latin--*Syzygium cumini*.

Six types of it are:
1. *Mahaphala* used in medicine
2. *Kaka Jumbu (nidi jambu)*
3. *Kshudra phals (shujra jambu)*
4. *Hraswa phala (bhumi jambu)*
5. *Golakara phala (gulab jamoon)*
6. *Vetasi Nerale (sheeta vallabha)*.

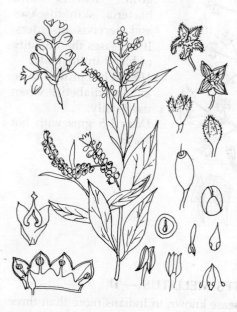

100 gms of *Phalendra* is composed of the following nutrients of food:
1. Fat - 0.3 gms
2. Iron - 3 gms
3.Carbohydrate -
                    3.5 mgms
4. Calcium - 19 mgms
5. Protein - 6 gms
6. Phosphorous - 9 mgm

Properties: It has a sweet and acid taste.
*Uses:*In case of diabetes mellitus either the leaves or the seeds of the plant are to be taken with honey.
Dosage: 1 to 2 gms of the dried seeds should be taken with buttermilk twice daily in consultation with an Ayurvedic physician.

DIABETES MELLITUS — III

Diabetes Mellitus is a disease known to Indian physicians as early as 3000 years ago. The important factor that promotes the cause of diabetes is leading an idle life with excessive intake of food without proper exercises. Before the advent of insulin as a treatment for this disorder, it was being treated by the Ayurvedic system of medicine by using mainly bitter drugs. In the ancient systems of medicine diabetes mellitus has been named as *Madhu Meha*. One such drug used for this with positive benefit is bittergourd.

Karavalaka consists of insulin. It is a recent research in the field of allopathic medicine, but our ancestors have been using it for diabetes since many centuries.

Its names in different languages are as follows:
Sanskrit--*Karavalaka*, Kannada--*Hagalakai*, Hindi--*Karela*, Telugu--*Kakera*, Tamil--*Pakarkai*, Latin--*Momordica charantia*, English--*Bittergourd*.

Composition of 100 gms.
1. Vitamin A - 200 I.U.
2. Vitamin B_1 - 68 mgms
3. Vitamin B_2 - 90 mcg
4. Vitamin C - 86 mgms

5. Fat - ¼ gms
6. Protein - 81 gms
7. Carbohydrate - 8½ gms
8. Iron - 5 gms
9. Calcium - 33 mgms

It is mainly of two varieties:
1. *Deergha* -- Long one which is bitter and white in colour.
2. *Hrasava* -- It is most bitter but it is small and green in colour.

Properties: It has an extremely bitter taste and is pungent in property. It is hot in potency.
Uses: It is used as a vegetable. It is used in diabetes mellitus with profound benefit. If it is used in excess it will cause aggravation of *pitta* and blood disorders.

Dosage: ½ to 1 ounce per day will reduce sugar in
blood and urine. This should be taken under the
guidance of an Ayurvedic physician.

DIARRHOEA

Children are very prone to loose motions; so also adults. They
resort to many other medicines but finally the cure lies in taking
a decoction of *Kutaja*-bark for a period of one week to fifteen days
depending upon whether either amoebic dysentery or bacillary
dysentery is being treated.

Kutaja grows in South India and Maharashtra and in the
Himalayan region. It is of two types:

1. Male *Kutaja*: Its leaves are small and its bark white in
colour.

2. Female *Kutaja*: The colour of the bark of the female variety
is black. Its fruit is small.

The names of this
drug in different langu-
ages are:
Sanskrit--*Girimal-
lika,* Kannada--*Kodasige,*
Hindi--*Kudaiyasa,*
Telugu--*Kodisaa Phala,*
Tamil--*Veppalai,*
English--*Kurchi,*
Malayalam--*Kutaka-
phala,* Latin--*Holarrhena
antidysentrica,* English--
Kurchi.

Properties: Girimallika has
a pungent, bitter and
astringent taste. It has a
hot potency. It is used to
stop diarrhoea and can
be given in the dosage of
5-15 grains. It is also
used in blood and bilious
disorders, skin disorders,

haemor-rhoids and when there is excessive thirst. This drug is used along with other drugs to alleviate vomiting, haemorrhoids, and heart diseases. Its seed is called 'Indraja'. The seeds of the *Kutaja* have a pungent, and bitter taste and high potency. It is used in gout, fever, diarrhoea and burning sensation due to fever.

Uses: It is commonly used for treating amoebic dysentery and bacillary dysentery.

Dosage: In the dosage of *Kutajarista*, a preparation of *Kutaja* is found to be very effective if taken one ounce with one ounce of boiled and cooled water, twice daily after food. The patient must avoid pungent and irritating food for a period of at least one month.

DOG BITE

Dog bites can produce rabies, and the treatment even with modern medicines is not encouraging to save a patient's life. However, in Ayurveda, there is a prescription by which he or she can be treated before the onset of the rabies symptoms. When once the treatment is done, provided there is no further bite from the mad dog, the person will not suffer from symptoms of rabies like hydrophobia and other complications. This should be taken under the strict supervision of an Ayurvedic physician who is well versed in treating such cases. The patients are strictly warned not to try the treatment themselves.

Ummattaka grows all over India. *Rajumathi* grows in Kashmir, Nepal and the Himalayas.

It has the following names in different languages:
Sanskrit--*Ummattaka*, Kannada--*Ummattigida*, Hindi-- *Dhattura*, Telugu--*Ummatta Chetta*, Tamil--*Ellapam*, Latin-- *Datura metal*, English--*Thorn apple*.

It is of two varieties.
1. White *Ummattaka (Lot datura)*; Alba *(White datura)*.
2. Black *Ummattaka (Fastuasa* black).

It is also called the *Krittaka Nakshatra* plant.

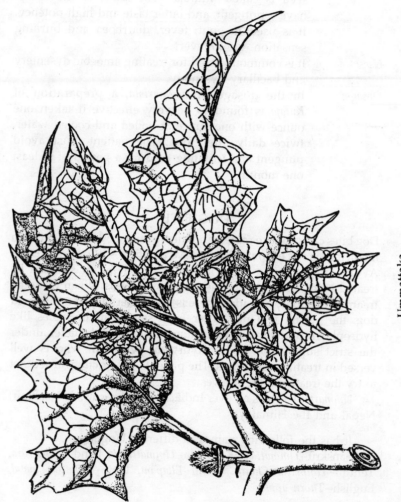

It is sub-divided into five types depending upon its varieties:
1. White
2. Blue
3. Black
4. Red
5. Yellow

Properties:	It has a pungent and sweet taste and hot potency.
Uses:	The seeds of this drug must be immersed in cow's urine and dried before use. When a mad dog bites someone its leaves must be ground into a paste along with jaggery, and til *(Calotropis gigantiea)* and then it should be taken internally and the patient should be kept under supervision for about 24 hours. During this period no food is given. After 24 hours he should be given a cold bath and buttermilk to drink.

DYSMENORRHOEA

Difficulty in menstruation is often seen in ladies during their menses. There are so many drugs, including hormones, being tried for this disease, but in Ayurveda an effective remedy is to use the decoction of seeds of *Til* in a dose of ½ to 1 ounce. This will not only relieve dismenorrhoea but also other menstrual problems.

Til is grown all over of India. Its seeds, oil and *kshara* are used in the medicine.

It is of four varieties:
1. *Swetha* (White)
2. *Raktha* (Red)
3. *Krishna* (Black)
4. *Vanyam*--forest variety of *Til.*

Its names in different languages are as follows:
Sanskrit--*Homodhanyam,* Kannada--*Ellu,* Hindi--*Til,* Telugu--*Gudbalu,* Tamil--*Ellu,* Latin--*Sesamum indicum,* English--*Sesamum*

Properties:	It has a pungent, bitter and sweet taste. It is difficult to digest, pungent and sweet in *vipaka,* and hot in potency. It is largely indicated in

Til

phlegmatic and bilious disorders. It is also a hair tonic when it is prepared with *Til* oil and used.

Uses: The seeds of *Til* are used to prepare decoctions to relieve dysmenorrhoea and other menstrual disorders.

Dosage: Four gms of *Til* is added to four glasses of water which is boiled and reduced to one glass and given at 6 a.m. and 6 p.m. with an equal quantity of boiled, cooled water for a period of 15 days along with a little jaggery. It not only relieves pain but also gives a good complexion to the skin.

DYSPEPSIA (INDIGESTION)

Dyspepsia is a feeling of indigestion in the affected person. The person will have no appetite and will have no taste for food. In such conditions the use of ginger, either in the form of a decoction or a powder, is advocated. The dosage is 5-15 gms or one teaspoonful with an equal quantity of water or with honey.

Nagaram (Ginger) is a drug commonly used in our houses while preparing chutneys, sambar and rasam. It is a powerful medicine used for different diseases.

Its names in different languages are as follows:
Sanskrit--*Nagaram*, Kannada--*Shunti*, Hindi--*Sont*, Tamil--*Inji*, Telugu--*Sonti*, Latin--*Zingiber offecinale*, English--*Dry ginger*.

The dry drug is called *shunti* and the juicy one is called *Adraka*. 100 gms of *shunti* contains the following:

1. Vitamin A - 641 I.U.
2. Vitamin C - 6.8 mgms
3. Proteins - 2.2 gms
4. Fat - 1.4 gms
5. Calcium - 2.1 gms
6. Phosphorus - 60 mgms
7. Iron - 2 mgms
8. Carbohydrate - 11 mgms

Properties: It has a slightly sweet taste with unctuous properties. It is cold in potency.

Uses: It stimulates the digestive process and also improves the taste of food. Its juice is taken with honey.

Dosage: 5-15 gms (1 teaspoonful) with 1 teaspoonful of water.

EPILEPSY

The disease of epilepsy was known by the name *Apasmara*, more than three thousand years ago to Ayurvedic physicians. A detailed description is available in Ayurvedic texts.

Golomi grows all over in India in wet areas.

The following are its names in different languages:
Sanskrit--*Golomi*, Kannada--*Baje*, Hindi--*Baj*, Telugu--*Vadaj*, Tamil--*Chatinam*, Latin--*Acorus calamus*, English--*Sweet flag*.

It is of four varieties:

1. Red
2. *Parasika*
3. *Malaberi vacha (Malaya vacha)*
4. *Chopa Chini*

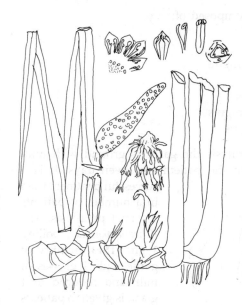

Properties: It is pungent and bitter in taste. It has a hot potency and hence it is anti-phlegmatic.

Uses: It is a powerful mental tonic and also good for the heart. It relieves distension of the abdomen. It is used as a memory booster, and for epilepsy it is given along with ghee.

Dosage: 100-200 mg with honey twice daily, along with 1 oz *Mahakalyana Gritham* at bedtime only.

FACIAL PARALYSIS

Facial paralysis will make the face of a man look ugly and the person affected will not be able to talk properly. In Ayurveda a simple therapy is advocated. One such simple remedy is the use of garlic. Hence, it is necessary to know the details.

Lassuna is a famous drug which lowers the high cholesterol content of the blood and thereby saves an individual from heart attacks.

The following names are used in different languages:
Sanskrit--*Lashuna*, Kannada--*Bellulli*, Hindi--*Lassun*, Telugu--*Telagedde*, Tamil--*Poondu*, English--*Garlic*, Arab--*Soom*, Persian--*Siyar*, Sindhi--*Thoom*, Bengali--*Rashun*, Latin--*Allium sativum*, English--*Garlic*.

There are three types of garlic:
1. Small
2. Big
3. Yellow-coloured.

100 gms of garlic is composed of:
1. Protein - 3.4 gms
2. Iron - 1.7 gms
3. Carbohydrate - 28 mgms
4. Fat - 0.4½ gms
5. Calcium - 27 mgms
6. Phosphorus - 309 mgms
7. Vitamin C - 13 mgms

Uses and Dosage: In facial paralysis the garlic is ground with milk and given to the patient for seven days. It is a successful treatment tried in a number of patients in facial para-lysis. The *Ksheerapaka*, i.e., boiling 1 gm (TSF) quantity of garlic with 4 glasses of milk and reduced to 1 glass, is given to patients of paraplegia and hemiplegia. It has been tried and found to be successful in 70 per cent of such cases.

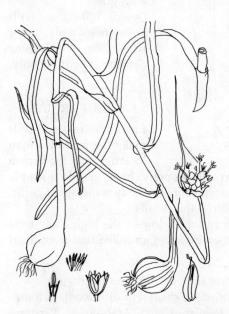

Garlic is also used while preparing vegetable soup, mutton soup and chutney. It contains 'Ethyl Sulphide'.

FRACTURE

A crack or breaking of the small or long bones in the body is called a fracture. Sometimes a fracture may even occur due to some disease. This is called pathological fracture.

Prithakparni is the drug that is used as an external application for the healing of a fracture.

This plant is grown in India where water flows regularly.

Its names in different languages are as follows:
Sanskrit--*Prithakparni,* Kannada--*Ondelehonne,* Hindi--*Pitavan,* Telugu--*Kolkuponna,* Tamil--*Kolapanna,* Latin--*Desmodium gangeticum.*

The protein present in *Prithakparni* will accelerate the ACTH (Adrenocarticotropic Hormone) secretion in the body. This also contains potassium nitrate.

Properties: This has a pungent, bitter and acidic taste and is hot in potency. It acts on the body and the mental faculties also.

Uses: In fractures of the bone the drug is applied with cat meat to induce the immediate setting of the fracture.

GENERAL DEBILITY

General debility is general or overall weakness in a person. There
are several drugs in Ayurveda which tone up the system. *Panasa*
(Jackfruit) is one such. It is used by all. It is very sweet in taste,
especially its fruit.

Panasa is grown all over India, especially in South India.

Its names in different languages are as follows:
Sanskrit--*Panasa,* Kannada--*Halasu,* Hindi--*Kathal,* Telugu--*Panasa,* Tamil--*Panase,* Latin--*Artocarpus Leterophyllus,* English--*Jack fruit tree.*

100 gms of *Panasa* fruit is composed of:
1. Vitamin A - 500 I.U.
2. Vitamin B - 28 mcg
3. Vitamin C - 9 mgms
4. Calcium - 20 mgms
5. Phosphorus - 35 mgms
6. Potassium - 400 mgms
7. Carbohydrate - 25 mgms
8. Protein - 1.5 gms

Properties: It is sweet and pungent in taste and cold in potency. So its fruit alleviates *vata* and bilious disorders. Its raw fruit has astringent qualities and is sweet in taste. It reduces bile and increases *vata* and phlegm. The ripe fruit is pulpy, unctuous and sweet. The ripened fruit helps in stopping bleeding.

Uses: Its fruit is a powerful rejuvenator and promotes strength in the body.

Dosage: 1 to 10 gms per day.

HAEMORRHAGE

Haemorrhage is bleeding that occurs in any part of the body. This kind of bleeding occurring either from the mouth or anus may prove fatal, if not attended to properly and in time.

The names of *Nagkesar,* which is a bud,·as found in other languages are as follows:
Sanskrit--*Nagapushpa,* Kannada--*Nagakesari,* Hindi--*Nagakesar,* Telugu--*Nagakesaram,* Tamil--*Velluttachanpakam,* Latin--*Mesua ferrea,* English--*Ironwood tree.*

It is of two types depending upon the colour of the flowers:
1. Black *Nagapushpavalli*
2. Yellow *Nagapushpavalli.*

Properties: It is bitter in taste, but is digested easily in the body. It is very effective and hot in potency.

Uses: It is used along with butter and sugar in treating
                   bleeding piles. To stop diarrhoea it should be

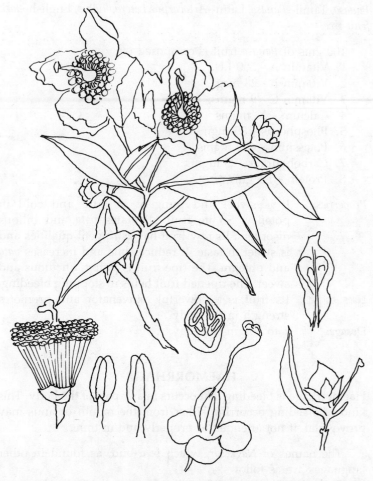

                   taken with buttermilk or *Jatiphala*. It is present in
                   Ashwagandha rasayana and *Drakshadi rasayana* which
                   are used for general weakness and *pitta* disorders
                   (bilious disorders).
Dosage: 250-500 mg, twice daily with honey or milk.

HAEMORRHOIDS (PILES)

Haemorrhoid is very common in persons whose jobs involve sitting in one place for a long time, and also due to constipation.

Soorana in the form of food preparation like soup curry is beneficial. This is a vegetable and is very effective. The details of this rhizome are given below.

Soorana is used only as a vegetable in our houses to prepare soup or curry, etc. It grows all over India.

Its name in different languages are as follows:

Sanskrit--*Soorana*, Kannada--*Soorana Gedde*, Hindi--*Sooran*, Telugu--*Mulshana Kanda*, Tamil--*Karula*, Latin--*Amorphophallus companulatus*, English--*Elephant foot*.

100 gms of *Soorana* contains the following:
1. Vitamin A - 400 I.U.
2. Vitamin B_1 - 58 mcg
3. Vitamin B_2 - 58 mcg
4. Vitamin C - 4 mgms
5. Potassium - 400 mgms
6. Sodium - 20 mgms
7. Phosphorus - 20 mgms
8. Calcium - 30 mgms
9. Fat - 0.3 mgms
10. Carbohydrate - 17 gms
11. Protein - 20 gms

Properties: It is light and dry, acutely pungent and astringent in taste, high in potency and pungent in its final action.

Uses: It is very useful in treating piles. It is applied as an ointment along with ghee and honey.

Dosage: It is used as *Palya/Chatni* in the food or as a dry powder, 1-2 gms with buttermilk.

HAEMORRHOIDS (PILES) — II

The patient of piles will complain of severe constipation and also an itching sensation in the anus, and bleeding will also occur. *Vrintaka* is the drug of choice. The drug should be fried along with castor oil and used.

Vrintaka is a vegetable used in our houses either to prepare *palya* or *sambar* or chutney. It grows all over India.

The following are its names in different languages:
Sanskrit--*Vrintaka*, Telugu--*Vankai*, Hindi--*Baigan*, Tamil--*Kattarikayai*, Kannada--*Badanekayi*, Latin--*Solanum*, English--*Brinjal* *(eggplant)*.

Composition of 100 gms of *Vrintaka*:
1. Vitamin A - 451 mgms
2. Vitamin B_1 - 52 mcg
3. Vitamin B_2 - 90 mcg

HAEMORRHOIDS (BLEEDING) — III

Piles are very common in people who have constipated bowels. If the piles are not treated in the early stage then it goes to the stage of bleeding haemorrhoids. It is the passing of blood through the anus. In this stage the use of the plant named *Mayooraka* is found very useful.

Mayooraka (Appamarga) is available all over India. The plant is usually one metre in height.

It is of three types depending on the colour of the flowers:
1. White flowers (6mm long), shining, greenish
2. Red flowers (*Achyranthes aspera*)
3. Blue flowers.

Its names in different languages are as given below:
Sanskrit--*Mayooraka*, Kannada--*Uttarane Gida*, Hindi--*Chichira*, Telugu--*Uttarani*, Tamil--*Naapuravi*, Latin--*Achyranthes aspera*, English--*Chaff tree*.

Properties:	It has a bitter and pungent taste.
Uses:	It is specially used in the treatment of bleeding piles in the body.
	Its *kshara*--alkaline water (one part of ash to be dissolved in five parts of water, repeated for 21 times)--and the decanted material is used for haemorrhoids.
Dosage:	50-100 mg with honey, twice daily.

HAIR TONIC — I

Hair generally grows on the body but especially on the head. It is a dimension of beauty for males as well as females. Everybody wants hair on his/her head to be black in colour for which sometimes dyes are used with different preparations. If young girls and boys want their hair to always remain black they can use oils containing some herbs. *Markava* is a famous drug used in Ayurveda for preparing oils for application on the head. It is contained in many of the preparations available in the market.

Markava (Bhringaraja) grows all over India in wet areas.

Its names in different languages are mentioned below:
Sanskrit--*Markava*, Kannada--*Garugoda Soppu*, Hindi--*Bhargara*, Tamil--*Kayakasi*, Telugu--*Galgara*, Latin--*Wedelia calendu-lacea (Yellow)*, *Eclipta alba (White)*, English--*Kadi Mulambit*.

It is of three varieties:
1. *Sweta* (White)
2. *Peeta* (Yellow)
3. *Neela* (Blue).

Properties:	It has a pungent and bitter taste. It is high in potency. These are the properties of the white variety.
Uses:	The oil prepared with this is used as a hair tonic.

HAIR TONIC — II

Hair is an important factor for the beauty of an individual. Nowadays hair loss is seen even in youngsters either due to deficiency in nutrition or due to the use of some adulterated oil. Ayurveda advocates medicated oils prepared out of herbal drugs (plants). *Iyandri* is commonly used in India for the growth of hairs.
Iyandri is available all over in India.

Its names in different languages are as follows:
Sanskrit--*Iyandri*, Kannada--*Havumekke*, Hindi--*Indrahyin*, Telugu--*Varri*, Tamil--*Peyakamalu*, Latin--*Citrullus colocynthis*, English--*Bitter cucumber*.

Its fruit is of three types.
1. Small sized *Iyandri*
2. Big sized *Iyandri*
3. Small variety.

Properties: It has a pungent and bitter taste. It produces heat after digestion. It is also hot in potency.

Uses: Its oil is beneficial in converting grey hair to black. It should be applied at least for a period of one month.

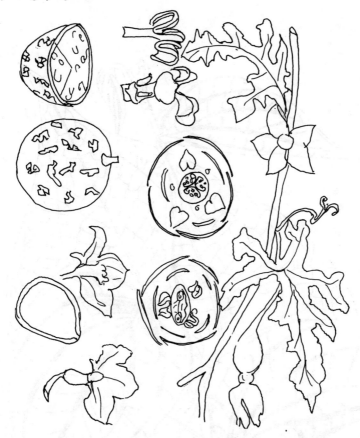

HEART DISEASES

Heart diseases are common nowadays, even though they were diagnosed 5000 years ago as per the ancient medicinal texts. There are several types of heart diseases. The present drug is very useful in treating congestive cardiac failure. It acts better than digitalis in the toning of the heart muscle, reducing the oedema and difficulty in breathing and other allied symptoms. *Tamboolavalli* is the drug of choice.

Tamboolavalli grows both in North and South India. Only its leaves are used.

The following are its names in different languages:

Sanskrit--*Tamboolavalli,* Kannada--*Villedele,* Hindi--*Pan,* Telugu--*Raaka,* Tamil--*Vetrilai,* Latin--*Piper betle,* English--*Betel leaves.*

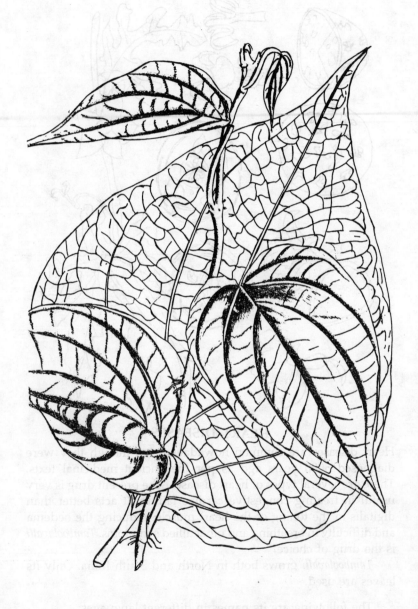

Tamboolavalli

100 gms of betel leaves consist of the following ingredients:
1. Vitamin A - 9330 I.U.
2. Vitamin B_1 - 68 mcg
3. Vitamin B_2 - 31 mcg
4. Vitamin C_2 - 3.5 mgms
5. Carbohydrate - 4.8 gms
6. Fat - 0.7 mgms
7. Protein - 3.8 gms
8. Phosphorus - 10 gms

Properties: It has a pungent, bitter and sweet taste and alkaline property. It is *anti-vata* and anti-phlegmatic.

Uses: It enhances strength in the body. It is more effective than Digitalis.

Dosage: It can be given in the form of *Tamboolasava*. One ounce twice daily with equal quantity of water after meals.

HIGH BLOOD PRESSURE

We are in the so-called civilised world. Frequently, we are drinking coffee on an empty stomach and taking food at irregular intervals in different quantities. We may not have a good sleep. All these may lead to high blood pressure. Even though in Ayurveda this is not considered as a separate disease, it is caused due to the aggravation of *vata* and blood. For such an ailment practitioners of Ayurveda have advocated the use of *Nakuli*. It not only brings down the blood pressure but also induces good sleep in the person.

Nakuli is called *Sarpagandham*, a famous remedy for high blood pressure. It was used in treating mental disorders also. It is also available in foreign countries in the form of Serpacil and its derivatives.

Its names in different languages are:
Sanskrit—*Nakuli*, Kannada—*Soothranabhi, Shivanabhi (Eshwari gida)*, Hindi—*Dhavalvarua*, Telugu—*Patalagandhi*, Tamil—*Chivanamalapodi*, Latin—*Rauwolfia serpentina.*

It grows all over Bihar, Bengal and Uttar Pradesh. It is of two types:
1. Small size depending on the height of the plant.
2. Large size.

Properties:	It is hot in potency, dry in property and pungent in taste. It increases the taste of food. It relieves abdominal pain. It is a known remedy for curing sleeplessness. It is used in treating giddiness, gout, epilepsy, fever and worms. It is commonly known as *Hridayavasadini* and *Kamavasadini.*
Uses:	It is used either as *Sarpagandha* powder or *Sarpagandharista* to bring down the high blood pressure to normal.
Dosage:	¼ gm to ½ gm and 1 ounce respectively.
Contraindications:	1. Low blood pressure.
	2. Pregnant women.
	3. *Shokhanmada*, i.e., insanity due to excessive thinking.

HOARSENESS OF VOICE

A change of normal voice to a disturbed voice is called as hoarseness of voice. This may be due to excessive singing or due to diseases like tuberculosis, cancer, etc. In order to normalise this type of voice a drug called *Abhaya* is used.

Abhaya is grown all over the world. It grows in India too. The skin of the fruit and the seeds are used for preparing medicines.

Its names in different languages are:
Sanskrit--*Abhaya*, Kannada--*Alalekaya*, Hindi--*Harad*, Telugu--*Karkkayi*, Tamil--*Kendakaji*, Latin--*Terminalia chebula*, English--*Chebulic myrobalan*.

Properties: It contains five tastes or *rasas*, except salty, and is hot in potency. It is very effective in *Tridosha vikaras* or diseases. It enhances digestion. It also increases the strength of the mind and body and tones up the sound-box.

Uses: It relieves constipation and hoarseness.

Dosage: For treating hoarseness of the voice it should be given in a dose of 1 gm with honey and for treating gland-ular enlargement too.

IMPOTENCY

Male persons may become impotent at an early age due to several reasons. In such a case *Vajigandha* is the drug to be administered.

Vajigandha is called in Kannada by different names such as *Angaragadde, Ankigadde, Angeruberu*. It grows all over India. Its roots, seeds and leaves are used in preparing medicines.

Its names in different languages are as follows:
Sanskrit--*Vajigandha*, Kannada--*Hiriya Maddinagida*, Hindi--*Aswagandha*, Telugu--*Pannerugadde*, Tamil--*Anukiramkalangu*. Latin--*Withania somnifera*, English--*Winter cherry*.

It is of two types depending upon the colour of its root:
1. White *Vajigandha*
2. *Desiya Nati Nonga-Praddhu*

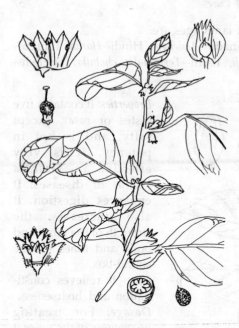

Properties: It is bitter, pungent and astringent in taste.

Uses: It enhances the strength and potency of the individual.

Dosage: It can be taken as a powder in the dose of 5-15 grains or in the form of a decoction. *Aswagandha Taila* is used to tone up the penis and the muscles.

INSOMNIA

Insomnia is sleeplessness and may have many causes. This is often due to excessive thinking and many other mental worries or due to high blood pressure. As a result a person feels fatigue and will not be in a position to carry out his work properly. Irritability and exhaustion are often caused as a result.

Jatamansi grows in Kashmir and Nepal. It is of three types:
1. *Jatamansi*
2. Aromatic *Jatamansi*
3. Small *Jatamansi*.

Its name in different languages are:
Sanskrit--*Tapaswini*, Kannada--*Jatamamsi*, Hindi--*Baalehad*, Telugu--*Jatamamsi*, Tamil--*Jatamamsi*, Latin--*Nardostachys jatamansi*, English--*Jatamamsi*.

Properties: It has a sweet, astringent and pungent taste.
Uses: It is a herbal drug which is used to induce sleep.
Dosage: It can be dispensed as a powder in the dose of ½ to 1 gm with milk twice daily, depending on the age.

Jatamansi

JAUNDICE — I

Jaundice is yellow colouration occurring in urine, skin, eyes and under the tongue. This is due to a defect or obstruction in the excretion of bile. The bile is produced in excess thereby producing a yellow tinge in different parts of the body. The physicians of modern systems of medicine in India refer the cases of jaundice to the physicians of the Ayurvedic system of medicine for treatment. There are very simple Ayurvedic remedies for jaundice. One such remedy is *Moolakam* (radish), the details of which are given below.

Moolaka or radish is used daily in homes for preparing curries, soups and pickles. It is grown all over India.

The following are the different names of radish in different languages:

Sanskrit--*Moolakam,* Kannada--*Moolangi,* Hindi--*Mooli,* Telugu--*Mullangi,* Tamil--*Mullangi,* Latin--*Raphanus sativus,* English--*Radish.*

It is of two types:
1. Small
2. Big.

Composition of 100 gms of *Moolaka*:
1. Vitamin A - a little
2. Vitamin B_1 - 58 mcg
3. Vitamin B_2 - 20 mcg
4. Vitamin C - 19 mgms

5. Potassium - 300 mgms
6. Sodium - 39 mgms
7. Phosphorus -20 mgms
8. Oxalic acid - 8 mgms
9. Calcium - 30 mgms
10. Carbohydrate -4 gms
11. Protein - 0-6 mgms
12. Iron - 0-2 mgms

Properties: The small-sized one is light in action and the bigger one is acute in action, pungent in property but without potency.

Usage: The juice of the radish is used for the cure of infective hepatitis. It has been tried on hundreds of patients with success. Even in the enlargement of the spleen, its juice, in the dose of ½ ounce to 1 ounce twice daily, must be given for 15 days. The juice of the radish stimulates the liver.

JAUNDICE — II

Jaundice is indicated by yellow colouration of the skin, eyes, urine and below the tongue. It is a disease of the liver and may be caused either due to adulteration of food or due to infection. In such cases the liver will be damaged and it should be brought to normal with the use of *Grihakumari*.

Grihakumari grows in India, especially in South India. It is also seen in the Arab and African countries.

Its names in different languages are as follows:
Sanskrit--*Grihakumari*, Kannada--*Lolisara*, Hindi--*Pinkter*, Telugu--*Gandhamanaram*, Tamil--*Katulee*, Latin--*Aloe vera*, English--*Indian Aloe*.

It is of four types according to its place of growth:
1. Grown near the Red Sea
2. Grown near Assam
3. Grown in Mysore
4. Grown near Jafarabad.

Properties: It has a bitter and sweet taste and cold potency. Only its leaves and its inner part are used in preparing medicines.

Uses: It is a famous cure for jaundice. Its juice has been tried in hundreds of cases of infective hepatitis with cent per cent success when these cases could not be successfully treated by the other systems of medicine.

Dosage: It can be taken in a dose of ½ to 1 ounce twice daily.

LEUCORRHOEA I

This is otherwise called white discharge, which is often common in ladies. If there is a scant discharge occurring then it may be considered normal. When it is aggravated and is profuse it leads to weakness and emaciation and also to a severe anaemic condition. This should be combated at an early stage by using *Kadali Palam.*

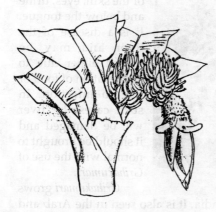

Vanalaxmi grows all over India. Its stem, flower, leaf and fruit are used in medicine.

Its names in different languages are:

Sanskrit--*Vanalaxmi, Kadali,* English--*Plantain or Banana,* French--*Bananier,* Hindi, Malayalam, Gujarati--*Kela,* Telugu--*Kade-lamu,* Tamil--*Kadali,* Kannada--*Balehannu,* Latin--*Musa paradisiaca,* English--*Banana.*

100 gms of Banana is composed of:
1. Vitamin A - 220-230 gms
2. Vitamin B_1 - 140 mgs

3. Vitamin B_2 - 28 mgms
4. Vitamin B_6 - 9 mgms
5. Vitamin C - 14 mgms
6. Vitamin E - 0.3 mgms
7. Potassium - 330 mgms
8. Chlorine - 75.4 mgms
9. Magnesium - 40 mgms
10. Sulphur - 12 mgms
11. Carbohydrate - 18.5 mgms
12. Calcium - 6 mgms
13. Protein - 1.2 mgms
14. Sodium - 8.2 mgms
15. Iron - 0.35 mgms
16. Copper - 0-14 mgms

Properties: It is sweet in taste and has a cold potency. Its fruit is sweet and astringent in taste and cold in potency.

Uses: Banana, *amalaki*, milk, sugar candy *(misri)* should all be taken together in the early stage of the disease of leucorrhoea.

Dosage: The preparation of medicine should be one gm banana, ½ gm *amalaki* and one gm of sugar candy *(misri)* with a glass of milk twice daily for a minimum period of 15 days.

LEUCORRHOEA — II

This is the medical name for excessive white discharge occurring in ladies. Even though several antibiotics and vaginal tablets are being used without any good response, the use of *Kaashmari* has given good results.

Kaashmari grows in the Himalayas, the Nilgiris, the Eastern and the Western ghats. Its fruit as well as its roots are used.

It has the following names in the different languages:
Sanskrit--*Kaashmari,* Kannada--*Shivanimara,* Hindi--*Kaayphala,* Telugu--*Budan,* Tamil--*Marudampatna,* Latin--*Gmelina arborea.*

It is of two varieties:
1. *Hiriya shivani* (Big variety of *Shivani*)
2. *Hrasva shivani* (Small variety of *Shivani*).

Properties:	*Kaashmir* has a pungent and bitter taste and is hot in potency.
Uses:	It is specially used in Leucorrhoea, and also in Menorrhagia, and Haematurea. Its roots and fruits are used.
Dosage:	Root *Choorna* 3 to 6 gms. *Phala* 1 to 3 gms.

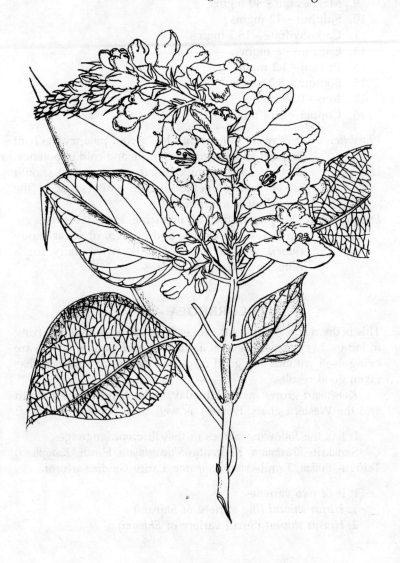

LEUCORRHOEA — III

Leucorrhoea is excessive white discharge occurring in ladies. Several antibiotics and vaginal tablets are used, often without any good response. The use of *Sadaphala* fruit along with milk is very effective. Its description and details are given below.

Sadaphala is also called the *Krittikanakshatra* tree. Its fruits, bark and leaves are used in the preparation of medicines.

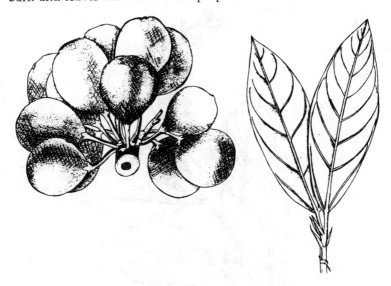

It is of four types:
1. The small variety
2. The big variety
3. *Kakodumbaritta*
4. *Nyadumbara.*

Its names in different languages are as follows:

Sanskrit--*Sadaphala*, Kannada--*Attiyamara*, Hindi--*Goolar*, Telugu--*Hedichettu*, Tamil--*Attimaram*, Latin--*Ficus glomerata*, English--*Country fig.*

Properties:	It has an astringent taste, and is sweet after digestion.
Uses:	This drug is effective in curing female disorders.
Dosage:	It can be given internally in the dose of ½ to 1 ounce with equal quantity of water for curing leucorrhoea or white discharge in females.

MEMORY

Memory is very essential for any individual, otherwise there may be many complications in day-to-day life. There are some foods which promote memory in an individual. In addition to this, in long standing cases of memory loss, it is advisable to use

called *Kadabhi*. Its seeds and oil are used in the preparation of medicines. These seeds can be powdered and used with ghee or honey.

Kadabhi grows in Kashmir and Punjab.

Its names in different languages are as follows:

Sanskrit--*Kadabhi*, Kannada--*Doddagunge beeja*, Hindi--*Malakengeri*, Telugu--*Bekkada Tege*, Tamil--*Valudai*, Latin--*Celastrus panniculata*, English--*Staff tree*.

It is of two types depending on its size:
1. Small: Its seeds and oil are used in preparing medicines.
2. Big: Its seeds and its oil are used in medicines.

Properties:	It has a bitter and pungent taste and is rough in property.
Uses:	It is extensively used in nervous diseases, and in treating a burning sensation and difficulty while passing urine. It improves the intellect and memory, and its action on the brain and mind is noticeable.
Dosage:	10 to 15 drops oil with milk twice daily.

MENORRHAGIA

This is excessive bleeding occurring in women during the early or final stage of menopause. This is due to excessive secretion of hormones. If bleeding is not checked immediately it may cause other complications, resulting in severe anaemia, and in some cases the uterus will need to be removed. *Kamala* (lotus) is used in controlling this ailment.

Kamala (lotus) grows in South India, Karnataka, Kerala, Andhra Pradesh and Tamil Nadu and also in some North Indian states like Bihar, Bengal and in Bombay.

It is of five types:
1. White Lotus
2. Blue Lotus
3. *Sthala* Lotus
4. *Kili* Lotus.

Its name in different languages are as follows:
Sanskrit--*Svetakamala*, English--*Egyptian or sacred lotus*, Hindi--

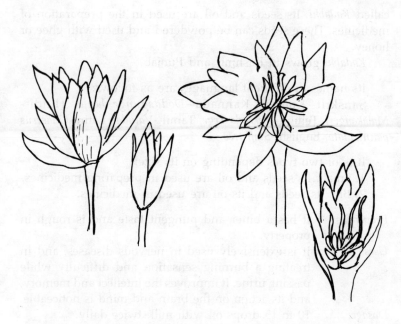

Kanwal, Tamil--*Tamarai (red)*, Malayalam--*Aravindam*, Kannada--*Tavare*.

Properties:	The flower of the lotus has both bitter and sweet tastes and is cold in potency.
Uses:	It is used to stop excessive menstrual bleeding.
Dosage:	The stem of the lotus has a sweet taste and hence, its powder is taken in a dose of 5 to 10 grains per day with ghee or honey.

OBESITY

Obesity is an abnormal deposition of excessive fat in the subcutaneous tissues, especially in the hips and buttocks, and in ladies around the chest and abdomen. This can occur any time in one's youth to old age due to excessive accumulation of fat in the blood. It may cause high blood pressure and lead to heart disease. Very few drugs are found in modern medicine for this disease. A gum of resin type called *Guggulu* is very effective in controlling the disease. There is a famous drug prepared out of this medicine called *Guglip* in a tablet form.

Guggulu (*Commiphora mukul*) is a gum of resin type. It is available in Maravada, Kathiyavada, Assam, Karnataka, Bengal, Arabia, Africa and Sind. In *Bhavaprakash Nighantu* five types of *Guggulus* are mentioned but only four are given here.

1. *Mahipaaksha* — It has the colour of a bee. It is useful for men and elephants.
2. *Mahanila* — It is blue in colour. It is used for elephants only.
3. *Kumuda* — It has the colour of a lotus. It is used for horses.
4. *Padma* — It has the colour of gold. It is used only for men.

Its names in different languages are:
Sanskrit--*Guggulu*, English--*Salaitree*, Hindi--*Gumguggulu*, Telugu and Malayalam--*Gugal*, Bengali--*Guggulu*, Kannada--*Guggulu*, Tamil--*Gukcula*, Telugu--*Maishakshi*, Gujarati--*Gugara*, Arab--*Mogla*, Persian--*Bai Jahundava*.

Properties: In property *Guggulu* appears to be shining since it is a resin. It has a pungent and astringent taste.

Uses: It is easily digested. It tones up the body. It is used for nervous diseases, obesity and wounds. The new extract is likely to produce obesity while the old one reduces the obesity. *Guggulu* must be used after it is purified. It should be dipped in a decoction of *Dashamoola* or else it can be kept suspended in *triphala* decoction. It is found to be an anticholesterol agent. So it also prevents heart attacks. It reduces obesity in an individual.

Dosage: It should be taken in the form of one to two tablets with hot water for a specific period as per the directions of the physician. The old variety is the best.

4. Vitamin C - 24 mgms
5. Oxalic Acid - 28 mgms
6. Sodium - 2 mgms
7. Potassium - 220 mgms
8. Iron - 1 mgm
9. Phosphorus - 60 mgms
10. Calcium - 200 mgms
11. Fat - 0.3 mgms
12. Carbohydrate - 6 gms
13. Protein - 1 gms

Properties: It is sweet in taste, rough in property, acute in action and hot in potency.

Uses: It is good in the treatment of piles. *Vrintakam* should be cut into pieces and roasted in castor oil before using it. It relieves swelling in the body and also pain.

PYURIA

Pyuria is passing of pus in the urine. It is largely seen in individuals who are suffering from venereal diseases, especially 'Gonococcal Urethritis'. Usually it is caused due to sexual contact

with the opposite sex who is infected with this disease. *Kan-kollakam* is largely used in curing this disease.

Kankollakam is not available in our country. But it is available in Sumatra and Malaya. Only its fruit is used in the preparation of medicines.

Its names in different languages are:

Sanskrit--*Kankollakam*, Kannada--*Balamenasu*, Hindi--*Kababchini*, Tamil--*Vilamelake*, Latin--*Piper cubeba*, English--*Cubab*.

Properties:	It is pungent, bitter and hot in potency.
Uses:	It should be used in the form of a decoction in an empty stomach.
Dosage:	One cup of milk, 3 cups of water, one gm of the powder of *Kankollakam* boiled and reduced to one cup should be taken--half a cup in the morning and half in the evening.

RETENTION OF URINE — I

Retention of urine is due to many diseases of the blood and also due to a kidney disorder, urinary disorder, urethral disorder, or bladder disorder. *Yagna* is largely used in relieving the retention of urine. The roots of the grass are used in this case.

Yagna is a grass which grows on the edges of rivers as well as near ponds. It is of two types, depending upon its roughness and smoothness.

Its name in different languages are as follows:

Sanskrit--*Yagnyanga*, Kannada--*Darbe*, Hindi--*Kush*, Telugu--*Babhahi*, Tamil--*Kusam*, Latin--*Desmosia chyabipinnata*.

Properties:	Only the roots of the grass are used in medicine. It has a sweet, astringent taste and cold potency.
Uses:	It is used in the treatment of urine.
Dosage:	3 to 6 gms, twice daily with milk.

RETENTION OF URINE — II

Retention of urine is due to many causes like kidney, bladder, urethra or urinary tract disorders. *Chandrasoora* is the drug for treatment in this case.

Chandrasoora grows in Tibet. Only its seeds are used in preparing medicines.

Its names in different languages are:

Sanskrit--*Chandrasoora*, Kannada--*Allibheeja*, Hindi--*Chansur*, Telugu--*Adite*, Tamil--*Adiviraji*, Latin--*Lepidium sativum*, English--*Common cress*.

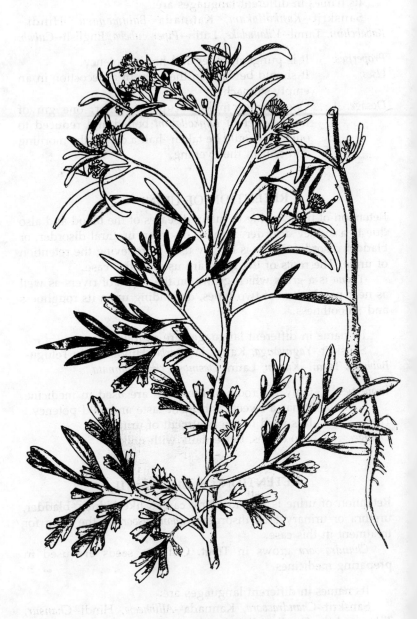

Chandrasoora

Properties:	It is light, dry and acute. It is pungent, bitter in taste. The seed is unctuous. It is hot in potency.
Uses:	It is a good digestive and carminative drug. It acts as a diuretic. So, it is used in cases of retention of urine.
Dosage:	¼ to 1 tola (11 gms), twice daily.

RHEUMATOID ARTHRITIS

Arthritis is inflammation of the joints. The patient will have mild to severe pain in the joints depending upon the stage of the disease. In some cases there will be difficulty in movement of the joints. The person may become disabled in chronic cases.

For such a complicated disease the treatment in modern medicine is also complicated. But in Ayurveda the treatment for such a disease is very simple and it should be taken for a sufficient time under the guidance of the physician. This disease is very common even in youth and middle age. If it is not treated early it "licks the joints and bites the heart".

Eranda is a famous remedy for curing *vata* and allied disorders.

Its names in different languages are as follows:

Sanskrit--*Panchangula*, Kannada--*Haralugida*, Hindi--*Errundi*, Telugu--*Aneidappachettu*, Tamil--*Aneamakku*, Latin--*Ricinus communis*, English--*Castor plant*.

Properties:	It has both a bitter and sweet taste and is hot in potency.
Uses:	In arthritis castor oil is given to lessen inflammatory swelling. It is given in rheumatoid arthritis along with ginger juice.
Dosage:	The dose is 1 ounce.

SCIATICA

Sciatica is a condition wherein the person complains of severe

pain in the region of the sciatic nerve. That is to say, one will observe pain in the back of the hip, thigh, calf muscle up to the heel.

In modern systems of medicine a patient is put on traction with a load or weight. It is annoying to experience or even see this pitiable situation.

In Ayurveda, this complicated disease is treated with a simple herbal remedy, called *Neelasindhuka (vitex nirgundo)*.

Neelasindhuka grows in hilly areas and near the seashores.

Its names in different languages are:
Sanskrit--*Neelasindhuka*, Kannada--*Neeliyahurinalakkigida*, Hindi--*Sambalu*, Telugu--*Tellavavili*, Tamil--*Vennocchi*, Latin--*Vitex nirgundo*, English--*Fine-leaved chaste.*

It is of two types, depending on the colour:
1. White and
2. Blue.
Its roots and leaves are used in preparing medicines.

Properties: It is pungent and bitter in taste, rough in property and it is also present in the blue type of *Sindhuka*.
Uses: In sciatica its juice must be given to drink. For back pain its juice and castor oil must be taken for one week.
Dosage: 1 ounce twice daily with water.

SKIN DISEASES — I

Man's body is always protected by his skin. Everyone wants his skin to be beautiful and free from disease. Whenever a person is suffering from a skin disease he is advised to use neem leaves and its juice and the oil prepared out of its seeds and leaves. Neem oil is used externally for skin diseases. In case of urticaria the juice obtained from its leaves mixed with ghee and *Terminalia chabula* is advocated.

Another famous single drug for a skin disease is *Khadira*. It is the best among the drugs known for skin diseases.

Pichumarda grows all over India. It is of three types:
1. Bitter variety -- Small Plant
2. Bitter -- Big Tree
3. Small one, *karibevu* (curry leaves), which is used in houses while preparing sambar, vegetable soup and chutney.

Its names in different languages are:
Sanskrit--*Pichumarada*, Kannada--*Bevinamara*, Hindi--*Neem*, Telugu--*Vepa*, Tamil--*Vembu*, Latin--*Azadirachta indica*, English--*Margosa tree.*

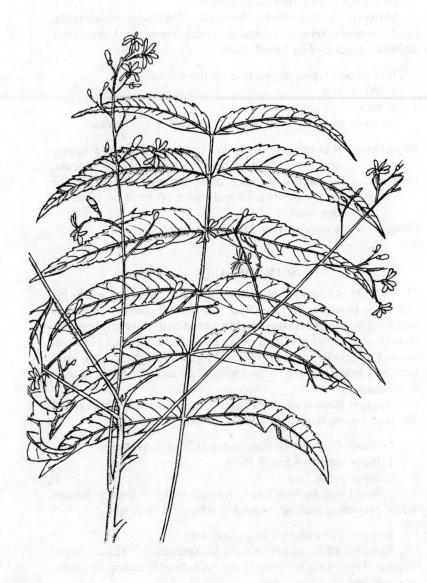

The leaves, root, bark, flowers and seeds are used in the preparation of medicine.

Properties: It is bitter in taste and cold in potency and light in property.

Uses: It is a famous medicine for skin diseases. The neem oil is used for skin diseases as an external application.

Dosage: The juice of the leaves can also be used internally, 10 ml to 25 ml with water.

SKIN DISEASES — II

Skin diseases are generally caused due to unsatisfactory and improper hygienic conditions and activities. The most common skin diseases are Scabies and Ringworm. *Kashmira* is the drug of choice for these conditions. This can be applied in the form of an oil or used internally as a powder.

Kashmira grows in Kashmir, Iran and Spain. The petals of the flowers are used.

Its name in different languages are as below:

Sanskrit--*Kashmira,* Kannada--*Kumkum Kesari,* Hindi--*Jaffron,* Telugu--*Kumkum,* Tamil--*Kongamalu,* Latin--*Crocus sativus,* English--*Saffron.*

It is mainly of three types.

1. *Kashmira* is available in Kashmir. *Padmagandhi* is stated to be the best.

2. *Bhaalik* -- It is white in colour.

3. *Paarasik* -- *Kumkum* is a little white. This is a good variety.

Properties: Kashmira has a pungent and bitter taste and is hot in potency. It is extremely fragrant.

Uses: It is used for treating scabies and other skin
              diseases. The oil in *Kashmira* is applied externally
              or used internally as a powder.

Dosage: 200 to 400 mg with honey twice daily.

SKIN DISEASES -- III

Skin diseases are very common in almost all underdeveloped and
developing countries where regular bathing is not feasible. It leads
to many skin disorders including scabies, impetigo, ringworm

and so on. For such disorders in the Ayurvedic system of medicine *Tuvarakam* called *Chaulmoogra* is used. It was commonly used for any skin disorder before the discovery of antibiotics.

Tuvarakam is also called *Janglibaadami*. It is grown in South India in the Eastern Ghats, in North Travancore and in Bengal.

Its names in different languages are:

Sanskrit--*Tuvarakam*, Kannada--*Garudaphala*, Hindi--*Papeeta*, Telugu--*Adavi Baadaavi*, Tamil--*Maravitakayi*, Latin--*Hydnocarpus laurifolia*, English--*Chaulamogra*.

Properties:	*Chaulmoogra* has an astringent taste and hot potency. The oil extracted from its seeds is used in preparing medicines.
Uses:	It is used in treating skin diseases. Its oil is applied externally in such cases.

SKIN DISEASES — IV

Skin diseases are often due to uncleanliness, not taking baths, using dirty clothes and taking foul food. *Chaturangulam* is a drug used internally and externally for such conditions.

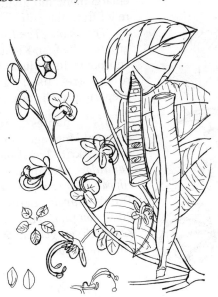

Chaturangulam grows all over India. Its root, bark, flowers, leaves and fruits are used in medicine.

It is mainly of two types:

1. The small variety and

2. The big variety.

Its names in different languages are:

Sanskrit--*Chaturangula,* Kannada--*Hiriya Kakkeyamara,* Hindi--*Amatthanus,* Telugu--*Rellikai Chettu,* Tamil--*Koraikayai,* Latin--*Cassia fistula,* English--*Purging Cassia.*

Properties:	It has both a sweet and a bitter taste. It produces loose stools as it is hot in potency. It is indicated in fever, *prameha* (urinary disorders) and mainly in skin diseases.
Uses:	It is used for treating all types of skin diseases, both internally and externally.
Dosage:	The bark is powdered and made into a paste and externally applied.
	The dosage given is 4 to 8 gms.

SPLEEN ENLARGEMENT

Enlargement of the spleen is generally seen along with malaria, jaundice and blood disorders. The patient feels pain in the left part of the abdomen. The spleen enlarges towards the umbilicus. *Teekshana Tandula* is the drug recommended for reducing spleen enlargement and giving relief from the pain.

Teekshana Tandula grows in Bengal, Kerala and Bihar. Its fruits and roots are used in preparing medicines.

Its names in different languages are:
Sanskrit--*Teekshana Tandula,* Kannada--*Hippali,* Telugu--*Pipula,* Tamil--*Tippali,* Latin--*Piper longum,* Hindi--*Kalimirch or gol mirch,* English--*Pepper.*

Types of *Hippali*
1. Big
2. Small
3. Elephant
4. Simhala
5. Forest.

Properties: It has a pungent and sweet taste. It has a cold potency and unctuous property.

Uses: A decoction of *Hippali* is given in conditions like enlargement of the spleen. It is noted as the famous *Pippali rasayana*.

Dosage: Its dose must be taken under the guidance of an Ayurvedic physician with milk and ghee as a part of the patient's diet.
150 to 300 mg. per day twice daily with honey.

SPRUE

Sprue is a disorder of digestion. In the presence of sprue the patient complains of constipation alternated with diarrhoea and

pain in the abdomen. For such patients there is a hope of cure by the Ayurvedic system of medicine. The use of *Madhuca indica* in the form of a powder 1-5 gms with buttermilk or in the form of *Arista Madhavarista* or *Madhavasava* in a dose of one ounce with an equal quantity of water is advised twice daily.

Its names in different languages are as follows:
Sanskrit--*Madhupushpaka*, Kannada--*Hippeyagida*, Hindi--*Mahuva*, Telugu--*Eppachettu*, Tamil--*Ellupi*, Latin--*Bassia latifolia (Madhuca indica)*, English--*Indian butter tree*.

It is grown all over India, especially in Karnataka, Bombay, Madhya Pradesh, Bengal, South India and Lanka. Its flowers, fruits, bark, seeds, *tila* (oil) and leaves are all used in the preparation of medicines.

Properties:	It is sweet in taste, cold in potency; it alleviates bilious and burning sensations. It increases strength and virility in the body. Its decoction is used to wash ulcers. It is also effective in phlegmatic and nervous disorders. It is a heart tonic and the weight of the body will be increased by its use.
Uses:	In the case of diarrhoea and bacillary dysentery its bark is to be powdered and given in a dose of 2-5 gms twice daily for a fortnight.
Dosage:	In a sprue syndrome the preparations of *Madhookarista* or *Madhvasava* are used in a dose of one ounce with an equal quantity of boiled, cooled water, twice daily, after meals, or 2-5 gms twice daily with hot water.

THIRST

Thirst is commonly seen in individuals who are in the habit of doing exercises in excess and also in persons who work in hot climates. This is a common symptom seen in diabetes mellitus. In order to quench our thirst we generally use the juice of the sugarcane. But this juice should not be used in diabetes mellitus.

Sugarcane is grown all over India. Its stem and roots are used in the preparation of medicines.

It is of five varieties:
1. White *(Sita)*
2. Patapati *(Pundresha)*
3. Rasamalae *(Karmakekshu)*
4. Black *(Krishna)*
5. Red *(Raktaha)*.

Sugarcane

Its names in different languages are:

Sanskrit--*Karkotica,* Kannada--*Kabbu,* Hindi--*Ganna,* Tamil--*Karambu Ekku,* Telugu--*Cheraka,* Latin--*Saharum officinarum,* English--*Sugarcane.*

100 gms of sugarcane consists of the following nutrients:
1. Vitamin A - 180 I.U.
2. Vitamin B_1 - 10 mcg
3. Carbohydrate - 52 gms
4. Calcium - 70 mgms
5. Protein - 0.3 mgms
6. Fat - 0.3 mgms

Properties: *Rasadale* variety has a slightly saltish taste.
Uses: Its juice gives strength to the body. It increases the output of urine.
Dosage: 20 to 30 ml.

URETHRITIS

Urethritis is the inflammation of the urethra due to several causes including infection. The patient experiences difficulty in passing urine. Sometimes there may be passing of pus in the urine. The drug recommended for this disease is *Trapusa.*

Trapusa grows all over India.

Its names in different languages are:

Sanskrit--*Trapusa,* Kannada--*Southekaaye,* Hindi--*Kheera,* Bengali--*Sasha,* Marathi--*Tavose,* Gujarati--*Tarnsali,* Tamil-- *Velrikayi,* Telugu--*Ujjakaayipa,* Latin--*Cucumis sativus,* English--*Common cucumber.*

100 gms of *Trapusa* consists of the following:
1. Vitamin A - Little
2. Vitamin B_1 - 27 mcg
3. Vitamin B_2 - 3 mcg
4. Vitamin C - 7 mcg
5. Calcium - 13 mgms
6. Phosphorus - 25 mgms
7. Iron - 1 mgms
8. Sulphur - 5 mgms
9. Fat - 0.4 mgms
10. Carbohydrate - 2 mgms
11. Protein - 0.3gms

Properties:	*Trapusa* has a dry and light property. It is sweet in action. Its potency is cold.
Uses:	It can be safely used in Urethritis where passing of urine is difficult. Its seeds help in producing more urine.
Dosage:	The extract of the drug in a dose of 2-3 teaspoonfuls and the powder of the seed in a dose of 1-3 gms are used in urethral conditions.

URINARY DISORDERS

Urinary disorders are very common these days as people do not take enough fluids, and acidity of urine makes them very prone to infection. The *Swetha Chandana* (white) variety of Sandalwood is used in the form of a decoction. The details of this are explained as follows.

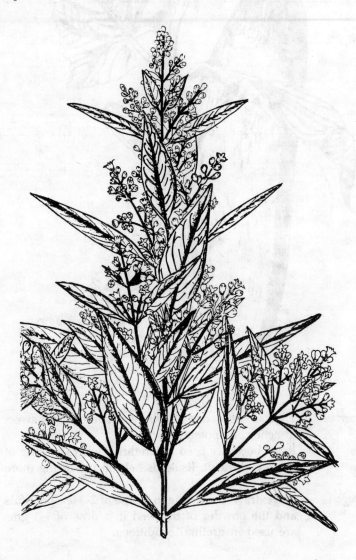

Swetha Chandana grows in Karnataka and Kerala. It gives a very good smell and hence it is used in preparing soaps.

Its names in different languages are:
Sanskrit--*Swetha Chandana*, Kannada--*Bili Shrigandha*, Hindi--*Safed Chandan*, Telugu--*Gandhuapu Chakka*, Tamil--*Sandanam*, Latin --*Santalum album*, English--*White sandalwood*.

There are mainly five types of sandalwood, of which, the white variety is the best.

Properties:	It is sweet and bitter in taste and cold in potency.
Uses:	It is specially used in urinary disorders in the form of *chandanasava* with water twice a day after meals.
Dosage:	Powder-- 2-4 gms, twice daily.
	Taila-- 5-15 drops, twice daily.

URINARY STONES — I

Urinary calculi are very common nowadays. This is due to the use

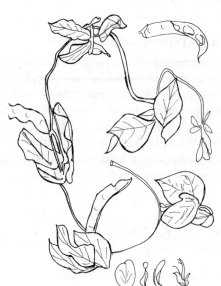

of excessive calcium preparations like milk in the diet. Horsegram is so powerful as to be able to break the urinary stone, the size of a lemon or a stone present in the kidney or urethra, and make it to pass with the urine from the body. The horsegram is used as a decoction or with any compound preparation like Cystone.

Kulatha or horse-gram grows all over India, especially in Bombay, Tamil Nadu and Karnataka.

Its names in different languages are as follows:

Sanskrit--*Kulatha,* Kannada--*Hurali,* Hindi--*Kulithi,* Tamil--*Kollu,* Telugu--*Ulavallu,* Latin--*Dolichos biflorus,* English--*Horsegram.*

100 gms of horsegram is composed of the following nutrients:
1. Vitamin A - 125 I.U.
2. Vitamin B_1 - 200 mgms
3. Vitamin B_2 - 189 mgms
4. Sodium - 30 mgms
5. Potassium - 300 mgms
6. Calcium - 250 mgms
7. Iron - 6.5 mgms
8. Protein - 20 mgms
It is mainly of four types.

Uses: It is used in the treatment of urinary stones.
Dosage: One ounce of horsegram powder with an equal quantity of water twice daily is recommended. The diet in the food should be old rice with ghee for a period of three months depending upon the size of the stone formed.

URINARY STONES — II

Urinary stone was found very commonly in individuals even as early as 5000 years ago. It is due to excessive use of calcium products in the diet and less use of fluids. *Trikantaka* is largely used in urinary stones as a powerful diuretic. *Trikantaka gritha* prepared out of this drug is a famous remedy for this disease (urinary calculi). The patient must be kept under a strict diet.

Trikantaka grows all over North and South India. Its fruits, roots and leaves are used in the preparation of medicines.

Its names in different languages are:

Sanskrit--*Trikantaka,* Kannada--*Neggilamullu,* Hindi--*Gokharu,* Telugu--*Panneru mullun,* Tamil--*Neru nagi,* Latin--*Tribulus terestris,* English--*Small calatrope.*

It is of three varieties depending on its flowers.
1. Yellow flowers
2. Red flowers
3. Yellow with white flowers.

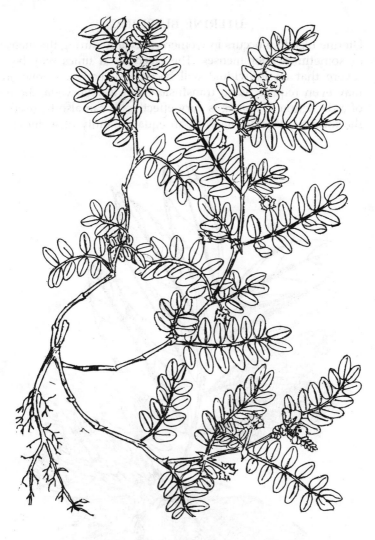

Properties:	It has a good taste and is cold in potency.
Uses:	It is used in the treatment of urinary diseases and stones in the urinary tract. *Trikantaka Gritha* is a sure remedy for urinary calculi. *Gokshura* coffee can also be taken twice daily.
Dosage:	The drug powder of 5-10 grains with milk, and *Yavakshara*.

UTERINE BLEEDING

Uterine bleeding occurs in women especially during the menses or sometimes after menses. The bleeding at times may be so severe that an individual will become severely anaemic and may even require blood transfusion. But in Ayurveda, the use of a decoction of *Ashoka* is very effective. It can also be used in the form of *Ashokarishta* with an equal quantity of water.

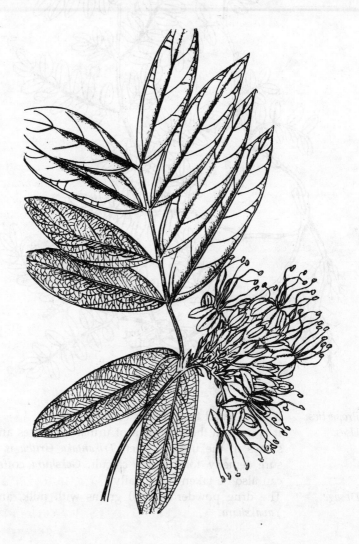

Ashoka grows in North India, Myanmar and Bengal. Its bark, flowers and seeds are used in medicine.

Its different names in other languages are as follows:
Sanskrit--*Shoka Nasha,* Kannada--*Ashoka Vriksha,* Telugu--*Kenkellimara,* Hindi--*Ashoka,* Latin--*Saraca indica,* English--*Ashoka tree.*

Properties:	It has a bitter taste and is cold in potency.
Uses:	The metrorrhagia and menorrhagia (excessive menstrual bleeding) will stop by taking the powder or decoction of the *Ashokanaasha.*
Dosage:	One to two ounces under the direction of an Ayurvedic physician, after meals twice daily, is the usual dose.

VOMITING IN PREGNANCY

Vomiting is very common in ladies during the early months of pregnancy. The treatment for this in the Ayurvedic systems of medicine is very simple and is explained below.

Kusthumbaru (dhania) is an ingredient commonly used in the house for preparing chutney and sambar, etc., and is a well-known aromatic flavouring in the house.

Its various names in different languages are as follows:
Sanskrit--*Kusthumbaru,* Kannada--*Kottambari,* Hindi--*Dhaniya,* Telugu--*Dhaniyalu,* Tamil--*Kothamalli,* Latin--*Coriandrum sativum,* English--Coriander.

The following is the composition of coriander (100 gms):
1. Vitamin A - 8,600 - 12,000 I.U.
2. Vitamin B_2 - 50 mcg
3. Vitamin B_1 - 48 mcg
4. Vitamin C - 130 mg
5. Potassium - 450 mg
6. Sodium - 3 mg
7. Calcium - 140 mg
8. Phosphorous - 58 mg
9. Carbohydrate - 4 gms
10. Iron - 7 mg

Properties: Its leaves have sweet and cold qualities. Hence, it alleviates *pitta* (bilious) disorders when there is a burning sensation in the body. When a person is having excessive thirst, he should drink cold infusions of coriander. This is also used with good results in sprue, anorexia fever, haemorrhoids, asthma, cough, pain and abdominal colic. It may be used as an unguentum, for *pitta* disorders, swelling in adenitis, burning sensation in TB adenitis. The coriander is a well-known drug which alleviates several diseases such as: heart diseases, vomiting, diseases of the eyes, and thirst. It has an astringent, sweet and bitter taste. It increases the output of urine. This can be given to children in the form of gripe water, i.e., coriander with water obtained from the rice wash.

Uses: It cures vomiting. It has been tried successfully in many pregnant patients suffering from vomiting.

Dosage: ½ to 4 masha *(old Indian weights)* or 2 to 4 gms.

WEEPING ECZEMA

In weeping eczema there is oozing, itching with small eruptions which can be noticed distinctively. Mostly this occurs on the extremities. The use of Betnovate or any other skin ointment and anti-allergic drugs or steroids have not given much relief. *Siddhartha* or Mustard is a commonly used ingredient in the kitchen in regular food preparations. This is very effective as an external

Siddartha

applicant along with *Snuhi* in the form of a paste. This should be used with *Kadirarishta*.

Its different names in other languages are as given below:
Sanskrit--*Siddartha,* Kannada--*Sasive,* Hindi--*Sarson,* Telugu--*Sasuvalu,* Tamil--*Kadagu,* Latin--*Brassica nigra,* English--*Rape seed.*

The composition of 100 gms of *Siddartha* is as follows:
1. Vitamin A - 254 I.U.
2. Vitamin B$_2$ - 70 mcg
3. Iron - 10 mgms
4. Calcium - 489 mgms
5. Phosphorus - 680 mgms
6. Fat - 37.8 mgms
7. Protein - 20.3 gms
8. Carbohydrate - 29.6 gms

Its seeds and oil are used in preparing medicines. Its seeds are also used in cooking.

There are three varieties of *Siddartha*:
1. White *brassica alsa*
2. Black *brassica*
3. Red *brassica rubra.*

The white variety is used to ward off evil spirits; the black variety harms the eye and the bladder. The red variety is used in the house daily.

Properties: It has a pungent and bitter taste and is hot in potency. It is used in gout, skin disease, etc. Its oil has a bitter and pungent taste with unctuous and hot potency.

Uses: It is used mainly in treating skin diseases.

Dosage: It is used as an external applicant in weeping eczema along with *Snuhi*. This should be internally followed by *Kadirarista*--one ounce along with water twice daily--for a period of one month at least.

WORMS — I

Worms are generally produced in the body due to excessive starchy food. For this, the use of the vegetable *Mahakoshataki* in the diet will not only prevent the production of worms but also in eliminating them from the body.

Mahakoshataki is grown all over India.

Its names in different languages are as follows:

Sanskrit--*Mahakoshataki*, Kannada--*Tuppada Hirekai*, Hindi--*Nenua*, Telugu--*Enu Gavira*, Tamil--*Gutti Veera*, Latin--*Luffa cylindrica*, English--*Bath sponge or Loofah*.

Properties: It is of two types:
1. Sweet tasting
2. Bitter-sweet tasting.

One is used only as a vegetable and the one with the bitter taste is used in preparing medicines.

It has the following composition:
1. Vitamin A - 56.41
2. Vitamin B_1 - 60 mcg

3. Vitamin B_2 - 9 mcg
4. Calcium - 35 mgms
5. Phosphorous -
          38 mgms
6. Iron - 1½ mgms
7. Carbo hydrate -
          4 mgms
8. Proteins - 0.3 mgms
9. Fat - 0.3 mgms

For the purpose of preparing medicines its flowers, seeds and leaves are all used.

Uses: It is commonly used to cure worms.

Dosage: 1 to 2 gm per day. It can be used in the preparation of curries or *sambar*, etc.

WORMS — II

Worms are produced in the body. They may be produced externally and also internally. The internal production of worm is evident when one is prone to excessive sleep and one's intake of food comprises phlegmatic production and inertia. This is very common

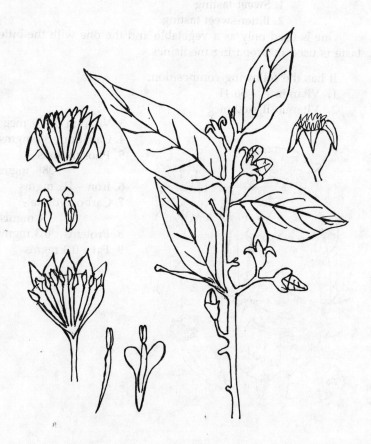

in persons who suffer from indigestion. Even the excess intake of starch and curds may also produce worms in the body.

Externally the production of worms is due to uncleanliness and also due to improper bathing which may lead to infestation by worms. In Ayurveda *Krimijagdam* is a very useful drug. It is easily available and within the reach of the common man and can be taken internally with one ounce of water twice daily.

It is necessary to avoid foods with a sweet and sour taste, curds and starch etc., in the diet. One should take baths at regular intervals and use clean and ironed clothes.

Krimijam is also called the *Anuradha Nakshatra* tree.

Its names in different languages are as follows:
Sanskrit--*Krimijam*, Kannada--*Agaru*, Hindi--*Agor*, Telugu--*Krishna Agaro*, Tamil--*Krishnagaru*, Latin--*Aquillaria agallocha*, English--*Aloewood*.

It grows in the Himalayas, Assam and Bhutan. Its bark and oil are used. It is of five types:
1. *Krishna agaru* (Black)
2. *Kalayeka agaru* (Yellow *agaru*)
3. *Kaastagaru*
4. *Dhaagaru*
5. *Mangolagarru*.

Properties: It has a pungent taste, is unctuous and has a hot potency.

Uses: It is used internally as well as externally.

Dosage: The powder ¼-½ gm of *Krimijagdam* is used externally by mixing with *til* or coconut oil for a period of about one week or ten days.

BIBLIOGRAPHY

1. *Ayurveda Remedies for Common Diseases*
   by T.L. Devaraj
2. *Charaka Samhita* by Chakrapani Teeka
3. *Dravyaguna Vijnana* by L. Aswathanarayana
4. *Dravyaguna Vijnana* by P.V. Sharma
5. *Gidamulikegalu* by T.L. Devaraj
6. *Glossary of Indian Medicinal Plants* by Col. Chopra
7. *The Panchakarma Treatment of Ayurveda*
   by T.L. Devaraj
8. *Mane Maddu* by T.L. Devaraj
9. *Sushruta Samhita* by Dalhana Teeka

Speaking of
AYURVEDIC REMEDIES
For Common Diseases
Simple Remedies Based on Herbal Medicines

This book is a handy, up-to-date and authoritative guide to the practice of Ayurveda, the Science of Living, believed to have been imparted by Brahma, the Lord of Creation. It contains time-tested remedies for the treatment of common diseases including jaundice, rheumatism and skin infections for which only Ayurveda provides a complete cure. These are home remedies which cost little, have no side-effects or allergic reactions unlike allopathic medicines, and are within the reach of all. Combined with diet and regimen, they not only cure ailments, but also promote health and longevity.

Contents
Foreword; Preface; Acknowledgements; Ayurveda; The Digestive System: Diseases and Remedies; The Respiratory System: Diseases and Remedies; Cardio-Vascular and Haemopoetic Systems: Diseases and Remedies; Fevers and Their Remedies; Genito-urinary System: Diseases and Remedies; Metabolism and Glands: Diseases and Remedies; Skin and Hair: Diseases and Remedies; Nervous System: Diseases and Remedies; Eye, Ear, Nose and Throat: Diseases and Remedies; Rheumatic Arthritis and its Remedies; *Medicinal plants quoted in the book; Major manufacturers of Ayurvedic medicines and formulations in India; Index*

ISBN 81 207 1611 6, Rs. 60

HEALTH & CURE SERIES

Positive Family Therapy: The Family as Therapist
M.D. Nossrat Peseschkian, 1995, ...1839 9, 352pp, Rs. 150

Psychotherapy of Everyday Life: Training in Partnership and Self Help with 250 Case Histories
M.D. Nossrat Peseschkian, 1995, ...1838 0, 264pp, Rs. 125

Oriental Stories as Tools in Psychotherapy
M.D. Nossrat Peseschkian, 1992, ...1071 1, 184pp, Rs. 95

Stress Management: Through Yoga and Meditation
Pandit Shambhunath, 1993, ...1514 4, 198pp, Rs. 70

You and Your Medicines
R.R. Chaudhary, 1994, ...1588 8, 120pp, Rs. 50

Overcoming Anxiety
G.K. Sahasi & H.M. Chawla, 1993, ...1461 3, 56pp, Rs. 25

The Pregnant Year: A Motherhood Diary
Monika Datta, 1994, ...1646 9, 204pp, Rs. 99

Stress: An Owner's Manual
Arthur Roshan, 1994, ...1673 6, 160pp, Rs. 70

Yoga, Meditation and The Guru
Purusottama Bilimoria, 1993, ...1478 4, 104pp, Rs. 45

SPEAKING OF

Alternative Medicine Acupuncture
Drs. Nilesh Baxi & C.H. Asrani, 1994, ...1774 0, 112pp, Rs. 50

Ayurvedic Remedies for Common Diseases
Dr. T.L. Devaraj, 1993, ...1611 6, 152pp, Rs. 60

Child Care—Everything you wanted to know
Dr. Suraj Gupte, 1995, ...1795 3, 232pp, Rs. 80

Heart Attacks
Drs. Carola Halhuber, Max. J. Halhuber, 1987, ...0261 1, 128pp, Rs. 60

Yoga and Nature Cure Therapy
K.S. Joshi, 1993, ...1360 5, 158pp, Rs.50

Sleeping Problems
Dr. Dietrich Langen, 1995, ...1773 2, 128pp, Rs. 50

Diabetes and Diet
Deepa Mehta, Dr. S.A. Vali, 1993, ...1048 7, 128pp, Rs. 45

Fitness Over 40
Dr. Walter Noder, 1995, ...1796 1, 128pp, Rs. 55

Asthma
Dietrich M.D. Nolte, 1988, ...0841 5, 96pp, Rs. 35

Healing Through Gems
N.N. Saha, 1992, ...0054 6, 144pp, Rs. 70

Nature Cure
L. Sarma & S. Swaminathan, 1995, ...0632 3, 232pp, Rs. 70

Yoga—A Practical Guide to Better Living
Pandit Shambhunath, 1995, ...1794 5, 198pp, Rs. 70

High Blood Pressure
Dr. Hanns P. Wolff, 1995, ...1772 4, 128pp, Rs. 50